M000004450

It is such wisdom as Daniel O'Leary's that will lead our people through this dark and narrow time in Western Christianity. God always sends us what we need. This is the wisdom that only comes from having been there, having done your homework, and having met God.

Richard Rohr on *Travelling Light*

To me, Daniel O'Leary is with Matthew, Mark, Luke and John in that he is fearless, always exploring, always confronting pain and hurt and trouble, and always finding and revealing these seeds of love and hope that shine like stars in our souls' darkness ... Daniel is a poet of God.

Brendan Kennelly on *Unmasking God*

Daniel J. O'Leary

TREASURED AND TRANSFORMED

VISION FOR THE HEART
UNDERSTANDING FOR THE MIND

the columba press

in association with
The Tablet

First published in 2014 by
the columba press
55A Spruce Avenue,
Stillorgan Industrial Park,
Blackrock, Co. Dublin
in association with
The Tablet Publishing Co.
1 King Street Cloisters, Clifton Walk, London, W6 0GY

Cover by Red Rattle Design
Illustrations by Eve Anna Farrell
Origination by The Columba Press
Printed by Sprint-Print Ltd

ISBN 978 1 78218 087 6

Third Printing

This publication is protected under the Copyright and Related Rights Act 2000. Conditional to statutory exceptions, no part of this work may be reproduced without the express permission of The Columba Press.

The moral rights of the author have been asserted.

Copyright © 2014, Daniel J. O'Leary and *The Tablet* Publishing Co.

Dedication and Acknowledgements

This book is dedicated to you who carry the seeds of a new beginning in your hearts – a new beginning for your own lives first, and then for the church and for the world. You are all, in fact, the human bodies and minds of God's own incarnate beauty, and when this revelation is growing stronger in your own heart, it is also growing stronger everywhere. It is important that you believe this. The dream is already within you. Now it is coming true. And other hearts are catching it!

In his *Evangelii Gaudium* (2013) Pope Francis repeatedly calls for fresh eyes and insight, for new and imaginative ways of talking about the enfleshing of God in Jesus, the Human One, and therefore, in every single human being that ever existed. And about how that transforms us and the whole world.

Treasured and Transformed is an effort to convince you that you are part of a treasured new beginning that is silently transforming you, and then changing the whole universe. Even one persistent possibility can wake you up for ever. Once your heart, soul and imagination are stretched by a vision, or possibility, they will never fall back to their old shape. They become the deepest part of you, the light in your eyes, the passion of your life. You were born for this moment to happen to you.

My thanks to all of you who have travelled with me through many years of adult teaching, retreats and honest conversations. At many Centres for Spirituality in different parts of the world we have been sharing the love-story together; weaving a beautiful fabric for our hearts to wear with a new joy. Out of this creative womb *Treasured and Transformed* is born.

Thank you also to Maggie Jackson, Sr Pat Carney CP and Margaret Foster for reading the first draft of this book and for making suggestions about improving it; to Margaret Siberry for her constant and empowering assistance and for agreeing to write the *Song of the Seals* reflection in Part Two; and to Michael Brennan of Columba Press for his passionate encouragement and support at those inevitable moments of doubt.

Contents

Part One – *Vision for the Heart*

The purpose of these reflections is to reveal the divine presence shimmering through everything when we pause to really see and recognise the deeper reality of things. This recognition leads to a transformation of our own lives, setting us free to live more freely, more joyfully and more abundantly. In the play of faith-imagination we recognise God's real presence in the present.

Part Two – *Understanding for the Mind*

Here we have some explanations and explorations of the graced habit of divining and recognising God's heart at the core of everything. They require a different kind of attention and presence on the part of the reader. The understanding of the head facilitates the movements of the heart. The chapters in Part Two are offered as accessible theological nourishment and spiritual encouragement, with practical examples from the worlds of art, nature and evolution, as we endeavour to become more sure-footed around the 'sacramental imagination' – that incarnational window of wonder through which we love to look. You, the reader, will benefit from reading these explanations, thus becoming more centred and confident in grasping and speaking about the meaning of this vision of Incarnation that underpins Part One – and, indeed, all my writings.

Introduction

Treasured and Transformed is about what happens when we live our lives in God's presence, aware of the divine essence hiding below the surface of everything human, seeing our relationships, our experiences, our sins, through the eyes and with 'the mind of Christ'.

Each piece in PART ONE – *Vision for the Heart*, begins with real-life situations, daily events or human themes and then, at the heart of it all, the light of a more profound presence is glimpsed. This way of seeing, this gift of recognising is called 'the sacramental imagination'. The veils of our often complicated and messy lives may then part to reveal a real surprise – incarnate beauty within us and all around us. That is God's secret, St Paul writes, 'in which all the jewels of wisdom are hidden' (1 Col 2:3). Part of that wisdom is the fact that 'You are God's poetry, written not with ink but with the love of the Holy Spirit, not on tablets of stone but across the pages of your human hearts' (2 Cor 3).

The work and play of faith-imagination is to perceive the deeper meaning of the ordinary, to touch God in the daily realities of our lives, to make the invisible visible. This happens when we try to be really present to what is happening. Simone Weil wrote: 'With imagination you don't have to travel far to find God – only notice things. The finite and the infinite live in the same place. It is here alone, at this precarious and vital point, that the holy is laid bare. I live in this world by attention.' This is the daily grace we long for. This is the transformation for which we were created.

PART TWO – *Understanding for the Mind* continues to work and play with the implications of the Incarnation, but this time concentrating on helping the reader to better understand some of the profound significance of the mystery of a human God, and of our own divinity. The aim is to enable you to know and to share more fully in your conscious mind what you already know in your heart. This will enable you to own the vision, providing you with a kind of spiritual and mental support and encouragement for practicing your own spontaneous ability to discern the deeper heart of all you experience. This background understanding of the beautiful vision of incarnation will work wonders for the wisdom you bring to every conversation, to every relationship, to every experience. One day this sacramental way of perceiving and of being will become like second nature to you, even though too often it will still be like seeing through a glass darkly. All will be revealed in heaven. In the meantime, we have to make do with glimpses. And with the work of reflecting the light of those glimpses for others.

The repetition of statements, phrases and insights in PART TWO is to help the reader to really face, grapple and better understand something of the beautiful Christian mystery of the Incarnation. Beyond just 'knowing something about' this mystery, the reason behind our consistent focus on its central wondrous meaning is to change people's hearts at a profound level.

Treasured and Transformed follows the pattern of two of my recent books – *Already Within* (2007) and *Unmasking God* (2011). Most of the articles in PART ONE have already been published in *The Tablet* (2010–14). PART TWO contains rewritten extracts from earlier books and new material. The thrust of the book is to open your hearts to an astonishing understanding of the implications of the Incarnation for your daily lives.

Part One

'Speak to us of God' the almond tree was asked.
And the almond tree blossomed.

Human Face of Divine Love

We need all the help we can get from the world's artists to get glimpses into what we mean by Incarnation, by the revelation that God's presence can be detected in everything and everybody, that there is a sheen and a shimmering of divinity in the most ordinary moments of our lives. There are special films that open our hearts to that revelation.

One wintry evening I went to see *Les Miserables*. I had heard about its spiritual power, its contrasting images of God, its compelling emotional resonance within the human soul. In particular, the words 'To love another person is to see the face of God' from the final song of the film seem to reverberate at ever-deeper levels in many hearts. People sense a profound truth in these words without quite knowing why. They hint at the unsuspected and astonishing closeness between the human and the divine, between heaven and earth.

To say 'I love you' to someone, some spiritual writers believe, is like saying 'Rejoice that your name is written in heaven' (Lk 10:20). In these earthly graces we experience the presence and promise of God. We are sacraments for each other, carriers of divinity, radiant with God's incarnate being. Such is the power of human love in *Les Mis*. Archbishop Emeritus George Carey believes that some moments in the film's story of the misery and ecstasy of human life contain 'the finest description of grace outside the pages of the New Testament'.

St John Chrysostom wrote that 'Whatever unlocks the human heart, unlocks the heart of God as well.' St Augustine said that 'The love with which we love each other is the same love as that with which God loves us.' When costly, enduring love emerges between people something new and beautiful is created. Every healing that love brings to a lost soul is a sacramental event. In all the aspirations of the human spirit another face of God is revealed. This is incarnate Spirit in time, place, flesh and free will.

The mystery of faith, correctly understood, reveals that creation, evolution and all the capacities of humanity for death and life are revealed as embraced, healed and transformed from within by the God of Jesus. The whole heart-wrenching story of *Les Misérables* with its extremes of tragedy, ignominy and despair, with its searing emotion and passion, its human endurance in the face of utter loss, loneliness and longing, is, in faith and fact, the incarnate presence of the Christian God.

There is no longer any competition between the world and God, between the secular and the sacred. The evolving planet Earth itself is, in fact, the body of God made visible. We no longer look up to the heavens for God; we now explore more deeply the human realities of our daily lives. Sacramental moments of intimacy with God are strewn all around us. These are the daily places of revelation. But we must dig deeply to divine the hidden spring, to mine the immortal diamond. 'What makes a thing sacred or profane,' writes Richard Rohr OFM, 'is precisely whether we live on the surface of things or not.'

With all its passion and power, its beauty, pain and pathos, *Les Misérables* truly reveals another face of God. It uniquely expresses, according to Rev. Dr Ian Bradley, 'the central Christian message of the redemptive power of forgiveness and sacrificial love'. Theologian Karl Rahner calls this way of seeing things 'the mysticism of life'. All our lives and loves are the work of God in the human heart.

God's revealed face is always specific and tangible; it is an enfleshing, an embodiment to be endured and enjoyed, reaching its fullness in one vulnerable human being called Jesus. God materialises in human form – the only form in which God's love can be experienced. Think, then, of the characters in *Les Misérables* and their roles, personalities, dreams, sins and shadows.

Into the three hours of the film so much of human life is compressed – the terrible despair of Inspector Javert and the aching loss of the mother and prostitute Fantine: the heroic self-sacrifice of the reformed Jean Valjean, culminating in the costly, beautiful blessing he bestowed on the bruised and blossoming love of Cosette and Marius; the youthful heroism of Enjolras, Eponine and Gavroche and the deaths they died for freedom; the unscrupulous gracelessness of the Thénardiers. Incarnation reveals the divine energy in all such human aspirations towards fulfilment.

But where is God in the terrible suffering, deception and cruelty at the core of the film? Jesus spoke of the divine presence in the criminals, prostitutes, drunkards and tax collectors of his time (Mt 25). So we believe that he embraced and actually became the hopeless lives of those urchins and prostitutes, the utter degradation and humiliation of once-beautiful bodies, the corruption and destruction of once-brilliant minds. Our wretchedly-human God still looks out from these ravaged faces in the rat-infested backstreets of Paris – or any other city. Can this be true?

Where can the real presence and promise of the divine be physically and mentally experienced if not in the dark labyrinths of human hearts? What is the stream of human desire that runs through the film but God's incarnate saving grace transforming that hell into hope? And where else can there be the slightest evidence that God is an effective, invincible power healing humanity at its most desperate, most diabolic and most despairing, other than in the raw reality of our complicated, ambiguous and beautiful lives? Every day of his life, Pope Francis will be reminding us of this resisted revelation.

'Les Misérables', 'The Wretched' – they have also dreamed a dream. They carry a relentless belief in the breaking of 'the chains of slavery'. The exultant strains of 'the music of a people who are climbing to the light', who are singing of those 'chains (that) will never bind you' in that 'new world about to dawn' sounds like a kind of secular *Exultet*, a redemption song of the people.

This vision of Catholic Christianity, though still not integrated into its full theology of incarnation, may be its most important contribution to universal awareness today. The freedom and the flourishing of humanity and of the world are the deepest desire of both Christianity and secularism. Human love and endeavour are brought to completion in God's heart. And they come together in the elegant theological line 'To love another person is to see the face of God'; dare we call it a kind of mini-credo of the Christian faith?

Beyond enjoying it as a moving film, watching *Les Misérables* through the 3D of Christian revelation is a moment of utter grace and wonder. Contemplation in a cinema.

The Hungry Heart

*There is a blessed and necessary intimacy between God and the soul
that too often gets lost in the more external aspects of religion.
The moment of receiving Holy Communion is the most profound
experience of that intimacy.*

In his introductory apostolic letter, *Porta Fidei* (PF), to 'The Year of
Faith' (2011), Pope Emeritus Benedict wrote about 'the heart that
allows itself to be shaped by transforming grace' (PF 1). It takes
intense love to transform a heart, that 'authentic sacred space within
each person'.

It is only from such heartfelt devotion, as the Pope put it,
'profoundly inscribed like a fire into each human soul', that people
become true servants and evangelisers of each other. That is why
he places the Eucharist, the feast of love, at the centre of his
apostolic letter. He writes touchingly about rediscovering a taste for
the sustaining bread of life (PF 3) and the *experience* of the love
received (PF 7).

But how can such a dynamic desire for a new and profound
flourishing of people's faith be generated? We need new imagery
based on the Incarnation, a new understanding of divine love
incarnate. Incarnation and Eucharist are experienced through the
human senses (1 Jn 1:1). *They* are the door of faith, the 'porta fidei'.

People grow in faith through their experiences – and our
experiences belong to the senses. Bread, wine and flesh are very

earthly words. They are carnal and physical. There is nothing ethereal or other-worldly about them. Yet wonderfully, these are precisely the substances and realities that God has become – first in creation, then in Jesus, and now in the Eucharist. In *The Great Hunger* Patrick Kavanagh wrote that 'In a crumb of bread the whole mystery is.'[1]

The utter humanising of God in flesh, bread and wine sounds shocking. No other religion talks about its God in this incarnational and eucharistic way. We are not saved by religions, doctrines, scriptures, pilgrimages and rituals. God comes to feed us – people of the flesh – in the earthly and unique intimacy of food. And we do not just look at it and adore it. We touch, eat and drink it.

The Mass is the Incarnation in miniature. Divine love takes the intimate shape of our essential, sensual and rawest selves. When we sit at the table of truth, immediately after receiving Holy Communion, we hear the vital assurance: 'I am now the living food of your flesh. I am the vibrant wine of your energy, the power within you. In me you are made complete, and you are invincible even in your darkest winter. And when your heart is full, it will overflow into the hearts of the hungry, bringing peace and hope.'

In his 'We Awaken in Christ's Body' St Symeon, the New Theologian, reflects on the miracle of Communion:

> *... and everything that is hurt, everything*
> *that seemed to us dark, harsh, shameful,*
> *maimed, ugly, irreparably*
> *damaged, is in Him transformed*
> *and recognized as whole, as lovely,*
> *and radiant in His light,*
> *we awaken as the Beloved*
> *in every last part of our body.*[2]

These infinitely intimate experiences of our sacred senses are central to the meaning of the Year of Faith. They purify and confirm our graced potential for recognising God's bread in every bread, God's incarnate body in every human body, God's own need in every need. And we do not just receive the holy bread; Pope John

Paul II reminded us in *Ecclesia Eucharistia,* we *become* it. And we become it not just for ourselves – as Pope Francis preached, we become it for compassionate service of others. What is most personal is most universal. We become it to light the way for others. 'Dear God,' wrote Blessed John Henry Newman, 'help me to spread your beauty everywhere I go today. Flood my soul with your spirit and light. Fill my whole being so utterly that all my life may only be a radiance of you.'

Nothing or nobody has the power to stop us from receiving Holy Communion – once we hunger for it. Countless Catholics, for one reason or another, consider themselves unworthy to receive at Mass. Or they are told they are. But the Gospels tell them a different story – that God is the freely-offered food for everyone, without exception; all we have to do is provide the hunger. 'Christ is the bread', wrote St Augustine, 'awaiting hunger.'

When we make the Eucharistic meal into anything else, something, for example, to define membership, we are on the verge of sinning against the Incarnation. 'Too often we use the Eucharist to separate who's in from who's out,' writes Richard Rohr, 'who's worthy from who's unworthy, instead of to declare that all of us are radically unworthy, and that worthiness is not even the issue. The issue is about surrender and hunger. And more often, surrendered sinners are much more hungry than "saints".'

We are all, in fact, forgiven sinners, hungry daughters and sons of a Mother-God who embraces us, nourishes us and gathers us around Her open table of divine/human love, and then, delightedly, offers herself to every one of us without exception. There was a passionate generosity in Jesus, an ache to be joined at his table by the sinners, the lost, the desperate. His only concern was about the attitude of the 'worthy', those who took his gifts for granted, the hypocrites who were smug – but not really hungry.

God's extraordinary love for us has never, because of a fall – original or personal – dimmed or faded in the intensity of its burning. It is in the ordinariness, accessibility and blessing of bread that this exquisite love incarnate is experienced and celebrated. And it is the *sacramentality* of the celebration that reveals a most comforting truth – in all our daily efforts to be human and loving,

Eucharistic grace is always surrounding us, enfolding us, empowering and consecrating us.

R.S. Thomas ended his poem 'The Moor' with these sublime words:

> ... I walked on,
> Simple and poor, while the air crumbled
> And broke on me generously as bread.[3]

Season of Soul

Without the gift of imagination it is very difficult to believe anything. In this article we are invited to the most sublime insight of faith – that the wholeness and holiness we search the heavens for, is, in fact, right where we are, at any given moment. It takes practice to perfect this perception.

I went alone to see the Palme d'Or-winning film *Amour*. I knew I would cry. Watching the relentless stripping away of an aging Parisian couple's energy to love each other was deeply moving. It raised the most sensitive issues about how we see loss, love and hope in raw detail in the most extreme circumstances. The cinema was utterly still when the credits ended.

Why was this, I wondered? Because, I suspect, we had been taken to the place of our souls, to that land where our deepest spirit lives – a land we are slow to enter. The context of our lives mitigates against such profound awareness of mystery. Too much un-happiness, anger, betrayal, fear and an existential and stressful urgency are filling our days and nights.

It takes great courage to set about regaining the lost rhythm of the soul. We generally postpone the work of self-realisation, of the inner journey, of the ultimate questions. Committed to a shallow agenda, we do not live at our deepest truth. We forget that if we do not live our lives abundantly now, we never will. And as death approaches we bitterly regret the greatest tragedy of all – our unlived lives. W. H. Auden writes,

We would rather be ruined than changed,
We would rather die in our dread
Than climb the cross of the moment
And let our illusions die.[4]

We need to keep resetting our spiritual compass so as to discern and painstakingly follow the innate, intimate longing with which we were born. Half-hearted hankerings after happiness won't do. Stifled though it may be, somewhere within us there is always a half-remembered memory of the way forward; we sense a vaguely familiar blueprint too often out of focus. It is hard to find words for this echo, this stirring, this blurred star that persistently attempts to draw, drive and sustain us, that reminds us of our true north, even while we fall back into the allurements of lesser lights and loves in the process.

The journey of a soul is never clear, direct or final. It tests our commitment to the limit. But distracted and confused as we mostly are, the original design is never lost. It spills through the cracks of our daily distractions, but it never drains away completely. Author Sheila Cassidy wrote:

And so we must begin to live again,
We of the damaged bodies and assaulted minds,
Starting from scratch with the rubble of our lives
And picking up the dust
Of dreams once dreamt.[5]

The required 'picking up' is no armchair rumination, no vague desire to be better. There is no self-help shortcut to the place of this emerging and radical vision. Old and shallow patterns of existence, of perceiving who we are, have to die for something beautiful to be born. It is not about proving, improving or accumulating anything any more. Nor is it about discovering some glorious plan or direction to navigate the labyrinths of the soul.

The truth of it is all so different. It is only through the hard and slow way of surrender, of unlearning, of reaching, through meditation, for T. S. Eliot's 'condition of simplicity that costs not less than everything' that the veils begin to part. Only then, beyond looking, can we learn to see. Only then, beyond knowing, can we learn to be wise. Only then can we commit to a life of compassion, contemplation and creativity.

The mystics offer us two inseparable signposts along the way of the soul – the vision of divine immanence, and the working out of it in practice. But how do we do this? How do we hold the sublime vision and the menial tactics together? The answer is hidden in the shocking revelation of the Incarnation – a kind of anticlimax we still mostly find unacceptable.

It is only in the loving vision and awareness we bring to *whatever* we do, the compassionate mindfulness that we infuse into the most mundane realities of our days, that the secret of the searching soul is revealed. And our work could then be described as love made visible. When we sense the gold in the rubble of our lives, when we divine 'the dearest freshness deep down things',[6] then we are living in the way of incarnation. And this changes everything. Our hearts begin to open, our eyes to shine, we breathe more easily, we face the dark confidently.

In his *Le Milieu Divin* Teilhard de Chardin situates this transforming awareness in the ability to see our ordinary lives against the backdrop of a divine horizon: 'We serve to complete [the creation], even by the humblest work of our hands ... With each one of our works, we labor, separately, but no less really, to build the *Pleroma*; that is, we bring to Christ a little completion ... There is a sense in which he is at the tip of my pen, my spade, my brush, my needle – of my heart and of my mind. By pressing the stroke, the line, or the stitch, on which I am engaged, to its ultimate natural finish, I shall lay hold of this last end toward which my innermost will tends.'[7] De Chardin goes on to say that knowledge is not enough. Love is the most powerful, the most unknown energy in the world.

It is also in the context of incarnate love that Fr Pedro Arrupe, former Father General of the Jesuits, outlines his agenda for soul-work. His words would be a fitting summary of Michael Haneke's *Amour*. 'Nothing is more practical in finding God than falling in love in a quite absolute, final way. What you are in love with, what seizes your imagination, will affect everything. It will decide what will get you out of bed in the morning, what you do with your evenings, how you spend your weekends, what your read, what you know, what breaks your heart, and what amazes you with joy and gratitude. Fall in love, stay in love, and it will decide everything.'

Mystic and philosopher John Moriarty's much-cherished words offer a comforting mantra for nourishing the *unum necessarium*, the essential focus of the soul:

> *Clear mornings bring the mountains to my doorstep.*
> *Calm nights give the rivers their say.*
> *Some evenings the wind puts it hand on my shoulder.*
> *I stop thinking.*
> *I leave what I'm doing and I go the soul's way.*[8]

The Grace of Loneliness

Where is God when people suffer the terrible pangs of loneliness? The pain when we lose someone close to us or generally feel forgotten by the rest of the world is intense but it may be a divine invitation to a deeper intimacy – the grace of loneliness.

Whatever chinks there are in the armour of our self-sufficiency, the cold fingers of February mornings and nights will find them. It is one of the times, over the years, when we reflect on loneliness.

In the seminary we were often warned that of all the losses entailed in a compulsorily celibate life, what would get us in the end would be loneliness. With hindsight, many of us would agree. Even fifty years ago in my first parish I sometimes felt as though I was pressing my nose against the window pane of other people's lives; as though a huge, holy and necessary dimension of humanity was missing from my own.

I once asked a very old monk at Pluscarden Abbey, Scotland, what he missed most during the decades of his faithful service. Expecting a profoundly mystical insight, his response surprised me. 'Coming home in the evening through the autumn fields,' he said, 'and watching the lights go on in the family houses and the blinds being drawn. I never got used to that lonely hole in the soul.'

Most priests are familiar with that strange moment when, after an evening of parish visitation, they return to their big, empty presbyteries. 'Loneliness waits', wrote J. G. Farrell, 'between

unlocking your door and taking off your coat.' Mother Teresa, who
felt the absence of God all through her life, wrote that 'loneliness
… is the most terrible poverty'.

There are many faces to loss and loneliness. One face is about
the precariousness of our human condition. The heart still twists in
me, for instance, when, visiting residential homes, I see the dull
glaze in the lonely eyes that once shone with delight – a delight that
fills the happy, faded, family photographs hanging on the wall
behind them. One such person admitted to finding the sound of
overheard laughter unbearably poignant.

There is an intensity of longing in those wistful faces peering out
from behind the curtains of small nursing-home windows. Are they
waiting for the return of a lost love, real or imaginary? Julia Copus
writes about an elderly woman. There is an ache in the image in the
last lines of 'Miss Havisham's Letter':

> Pray God that you will be here soon; the furniture
> is weary, my darling, of the name I am forever
> fingering into its dust.[9]

Such lovely people, often fighting against the destructive edge
of bitterness, still keep their parental hearts as full of love as ever –
and no one visits. 'One may have a blazing hearth in one's soul',
wrote Vincent van Gogh, 'and yet no one ever comes to sit by it.'

Because the human heart is wonderfully and fearfully created
with a divine compulsion to be given away and to be received, there
is an existential dread in us of the keen pain of loneliness or
rejection. Thomas Wolfe is convinced that 'loneliness is the central
and inevitable fact of human existence'.

There are many ways to break a heart. Ask those who, suddenly
bereft, weep for what they had taken for granted. Is there a soul on
earth that cannot identify, in one way or another, with Mary Jean
Irion's cry:

> One day I shall dig my fingers
> into the earth,
> or bury my face in the pillow,

or stretch myself taut,
or raise my hands to the sky,
and want more than all the world
your return.[10]

In words of unforgettable pathos, Andrew Motion's poem 'In the Attic' takes us into the terrible pain of loneliness and grief. He tells of the times he spent in the attic with the locked trunk of clothes of someone very loved and very young:

... a green holiday; a red christening;
all your unfinished lives
fading through dark summers
entering my head as dust.[11]

Another face of loneliness emerges from the state of alienation in which people today find themselves, being disconnected from their own bodies, their environment, their universe and therefore God. The psychic damage we suffer from such separation is all too clear because there is a loving unity that holds all Creation together. Whenever that is fractured, something dies within us. And the hidden loneliness deepens.

The Christian mystics have beautiful ways of describing the mystery of the intimacy of all Creation. Hildegard of Bingen wrote that 'God has built the human form into the cosmic structure; all things are arranged in consideration of everything else.'

Something intuitive within us senses this delicate dependence. The contemplative heart grieves at the greed that hacks across these fragile lifelines of universal wholeness. When this circle of life is broken the loss is great; the life-giving dance of the Blessed Trinity within us loses its rhythm. Nothing remains untouched by such deliberate destruction. An unconscious, existential loneliness is one of its deadly symptoms.

The idea is everywhere present in Jewish and Christian spirituality that the only antidote to human loneliness is to contemplate the face of God, to surrender to what is greater than ourselves – to recognise the beautiful love at the heart of everything. We must learn to adore incarnate wonder; to look at the sea and feel God's beating heart; under the moving clouds to sense the brooding presence of the Holy Ghost; to gaze at the night sky above a lonely planet and sense a secret birthing; to lose heart before the tears of things and yet to experience the sublime comfort of divine arms. 'Man's loneliness', wrote Eugene O'Neill, 'is but his fear of life.'

Divine Mystery has become utterly identified with the human condition. All our longing is ultimately a longing for God, and all longing is the longing of an incarnate God for us. 'God possesses the heavens,' wrote W. B. Yeats, 'but he covets the earth ... oh, he covets the earth.'

Beyond theological definitions, there is a fierce emptiness in God that only our freely-given loving presence can fill. In the end, when fully felt and accepted, maybe human loneliness is the divine invitation to the most intense intimacy of all.

Take Away the Carapace

*For many people their greatest fear is of public humiliation and disgrace.
But Jesus' own example teaches that such a stripping away of reputation
is a necessary purification and a way to grace.*

As he wrote out the prescription, the doctor said: 'Camouflage
cream should do it.' The pink vitiligo patches on my friend's face
would never be healed, he said, but they could, at least, be covered
up. As we left the surgery, we spoke about our preoccupation with
hiding all kinds of things in all kinds of ways at many levels of our
lives.

Institutions do it too. Issues such as the denials of politicians
regarding their hidden expenses claims, the phone hacking scandals
involving police, government and media, the Hillsborough cover-
up, and the revelations surrounding the Edward Snowden
whistleblower case carry a profound threat to the fragile grace of
trust without which any society cannot remain healthy and safe for
long.

Albert Einstein's astute observation that 'the last thing to
collapse is the surface' remains shockingly relevant today. When
the infrastructure of an institution is rotten there is nothing to
bolster up the structure. When confidence goes the crash comes.
The erosion of trust in Church and State in Ireland has brought the
country to its knees. And it all looked so good for so long – but only
on the surface.

Whether it has to do with our appearance, our popularity or the integrity of our organisations, we have a congenital desire to deny all flaws and imperfections. We tell lies, we scapegoat others, we sell our souls to save our face. Our deepest fear, it is often said, is the fear of being found out.

Like many others, I suppose I, too, carry a fear of public disgrace. At a time when so many of my brother priests are in the news for the wrong reasons, I wonder how I would respond to the charge of some crime. While the Sunday papers were blazing the details of it, would I turn up for Mass, as usual, to face the congregation? Or would I run and hide? There are thousands of us who silently worry about these things.

I remember a time when I experienced a small version of public shame. Even though it was in the context of a holistic and healing week, and even though everyone else there was battling with their own demons, it was still a shock to my system. My carefully crafted covers, masks and shells were ruthlessly removed, to reveal a very wounded, unfinished and unprotected inner creature. It was a classic moment of humiliation.

Our spiritual guides tell us that along the way of the soul, if it is to be a truly transforming journey, an encounter with some kind of public shame is necessary. In their search for enlightenment, the Sufis call this the moment of *malamat* – when discredit and humiliation happen. There is no purification without humiliation. There is, they would say, a grace in disgrace.

'I tell holy people who come to me to pray for one good humiliation every day,' writes Richard Rohr. 'And then I tell them to keep careful watch over their reaction to those humiliations. That is the only way you can avoid religious grandiosity, and know that you are seeking God and not yourself.'

When reputations are suddenly destroyed, for one reason or another, some people just cannot hold their lives together any more. Their souls are crushed for ever. There is nothing left for another beginning. But others, for whom the final dependence on human respect is broken, gradually begin to blossom in a new way. Something has been liberated inside them – a new and beautiful possibility.

The late Cardinal Bernardin of Chicago was a great and humble prophet of love. He had two deadly fears in his life – the fear of disgrace and the fear of cancer. After midlife, they both struck. He spent twelve months in pure pain when he was falsely accused of criminal behaviour before he was finally acquitted. His cancer was then discovered and he soon died. But during his final few months, having faced the two great fears of his life, he walked tall, his friends said, elegant and graceful, a free man.

My own brush with public humiliation carried its slow graces – eventually I felt it was a breakthrough into a deeper self-knowledge and authenticity. What took a beating was my ego. The ego prefers anything, just about anything, to falling, failing, being shown up. Usually it is a garrulous and devious tyrant, a confusing and ensnaring charlatan-self that usurps the reality of the true self, the God-Self.

'As long as we haven't unmasked the ego, it continues to hoodwink us, like a sleazy politician endlessly parading bogus promises, or a lawyer constantly inventing ingenious lies and defences,' wrote Sogyal Rinpoche in his *The Tibetan Book of Living and Dying*. 'Again and again we give in to its demands.'

As long as Jesus is the one we follow, then there is no avoiding the necessary humiliation in the painful stripping away of our vanity, our pretentious carapace, our titles, our reliance on a false and privileged exemption from the pursuit of inner authenticity. The outer shell must be pierced, the masks removed. Before it's too late, and if we are lucky, we may slowly and painfully discover our long deceit.

It was the hypocrisy of the priests of his time that got Jesus so mad. He just could not stomach their religious pretence. It enraged him. He had no problem with the outcasts, the disgraced public sinners, the utter failures and misfits of his society. Unlike us, he welcomed and healed them. But he could get nowhere with the hypocritical scribes and Pharisees who he describes as being like 'whitewashed tombs' (Mt 23:27).

The mystic Rumi's advice reminds us of the practice of the ancient Celtic public penances. Only such humiliating suffering, and our deepest reflection on it, will ever reveal to each one of us the *unum necessarium*, the one thing we were created for – the possession and celebration of our truest self.

> *Put what salve you have on yourself.*
> *Point out to everyone the disease you are.*
> *That's part of getting well.*
> *When you lance yourself that way,*
> *You become more merciful and wiser.*[12]

We grow into our true selves, not by adding more to them, but by stripping and emptying them of our addictions to power, prestige and popularity. What a dying it was for Jesus, and is for us, when our good name lies in smithereens around us. What is left in us when all is taken away? When our cover is blown, when the image is shattered, how do we look naked, ridiculed, crucified? It is not easy to look good on wood.

In the end, it all makes you wonder whether those shattering moments of public humiliation are necessary for the total purification of the human soul. They were for Jesus. Maybe such disgrace is the final grace – the last block to be removed, the last crutch to be kicked away, before we place our trust completely in the jealous heart of our human-God.

Kavanagh's Christmas

The Irish poet and farmer Patrick Kavanagh had an instinctive awareness of the meaning of incarnation. His was a sacramental imagination. Even in his descriptions of the most common things, his homespun words and wisdom carry in them hints of Heaven.

My father played the melodion
Outside at our gate;
There were stars in the morning east
And they danced to his music.[13]

In 'A Christmas Childhood' Patrick Kavanagh remembers a Christmas morning when he was six years old. His father left the 'half-door' open and made music near the gate. The boy's memories of what he saw and heard filled him with excitement. 'One side of the potato-pit was white with frost – how wonderful that was, how wonderful!' And later, when he put his ear to the paling-post near the front window 'the music that came out was magical'.

There can be few poets who have captured something of the mystery of the Incarnation better than Patrick Kavanagh. Everything he wrote about the most common things carried hints of heaven. A man of the soul and of the soil, he was a poet of the ordinary, 'smelting into passion the commonplaces of life'.

Surrounded by his beloved fields, hills and pathways, his spirit was not confined by them – only liberated into the eternal. Through simple and familiar things he came to understand the universe. Ploughing, spraying the potatoes, milking, feeding sheep, a horse called Polly, a farmer called Maguire, and 'three whin bushes' called the 'Three Wise Men' approaching Inniskeen – such were Kavanagh's earthly windows into an incarnate heaven.

> *Across the wild bogs his melodion called*
> *To Lennons and Callans.*
> *As I pulled on my trousers in a hurry*
> *I knew some strange thing had happened.*[14]

For Kavanagh, childhood, poetry and theology were all of a piece. His farm was his bible, County Monaghan his Bethlehem, his poetry was his prayer, and along the Inniskeen road he experienced his daily Emmaus revelations. Even his new long trousers were woven into the mystery. A natural contemplative, Kavanagh read God's signature in every face of nature; he expected angels to appear 'round the bends of old roads'.

In his novel *Tarry Flynn* the son returns from a day's work on the farm and tells his aging mother, 'The Holy Ghost is in the fields.' Confused, his mother asks him, 'Is it something to do with the Catholic religion you mean?' Her son assures her that 'It is something to do with every religion.'

> *Outside in the cow-house my mother*
> *Made the music of milking;*
> *The light of her stable-lamp was a star*
> *And the frost of Bethlehem made it twinkle.*[15]

Though reared in a grim climate of poverty and survival, Kavanagh's imagination flourished. He had no fear of a punishing God. For him, the Maker of an astonishing Creation could only be a beautiful and loving God, a tender Mother who 'caresses the daily and nightly earth'. The miracle of continuing creation, of the renewal of the world each day and each season, filled him with a child's wonder. 'And in the green meadows', he wrote, 'the maiden of spring is with child through the Holy Ghost.'

Kavanagh believed in a God of healing more than in a God of unlimited power, a God whose beauty was reflected more purely in the soft shape of a bluebell than in the hard face of the Catholic Church of his time. Though often described as a rough and rustic neighbour, he had an exquisitely childlike understanding of God's unconditional love. Kavanagh felt this profoundly when recovering from lung-cancer surgery in 1954. While walking alongside Dublin's Grand Canal he experienced, in ordinary sights and sounds, the renewal of his spiritual and bodily health. 'The green waters of the canal were pouring redemption on me,' he wrote.

From the beginning an intuitive awareness of the deeper meaning of incarnation filled his soul. Everything spoke to him of the mystery and holiness of our lives. His most quoted verse is

> *God is in the bits and pieces of Every Day –*
> *A kiss here and a laugh again, and sometimes tears,*
> *A pearl necklace round the neck of poverty.*[16]

Dominican Brother Tom Casey, a farmer and a bit of a poet himself, is a great fan of Patrick Kavanagh. 'Like all great poets,' Brother Tom said to me, 'Kavanagh invites us to look at the world and to see beauty in the things we take for granted. But he does more than that: he goes beneath the beauty and shows us the inner meaning.' Until one day we will finally recognise the face of our incarnate God of surprises and disguises everywhere.

When Kavanagh writes of his little bedroom only 'ten by twelve', with its sloping roof so low he cannot stand, he knows it's nothing more than a dusty attic. 'But its little window lets in the stars.' Here we have the sacramental imagination at its best. We find it again in his much-loved 'The One' where he tells the local farmers, 'That beautiful, beautiful, beautiful God was breathing His love by a cut-away bog.'[17]

> *My father played the melodion,*
> *My mother milked the cows,*
> *And I had a prayer like a white rose pinned*
> *On the Virgin Mary's blouse.*[18]

Kavanagh's sacramentalising imagination around incarnation heard 'the cry of things young and elemental' everywhere, and, as a child, each visit to the uncultivated patch of wild weeds at the back of his house 'where sows root and hens scratch' was like 'dipping his fingers in the pockets of God'. Those pockets were his five senses. And they were never empty. He reminds us, in his poem 'Advent', that when the Christmas carols are over, the incarnate melody of the daily psalm begins – the music of what happens.

> We'll hear it in the whispered argument of a churning
> Or in the streets where the village boys are lurching.
> And we'll hear it among simple, decent men, too,
> Who barrow dung in gardens under trees,
> Wherever life pours ordinary plenty.[19]

Holy Hearts that Know How to Adore

Those with Down's syndrome may not grasp the long-outdated philosophical concept of transubstantiation, but they receive Holy Communion with the utmost reverence and love.

A hot afternoon during the summer sales and Tesco's cafe was teeming. Overdressed and overspending, a perspiring woman bought a packet of biscuits and a cup of tea to calm her nerves. She spotted an empty table only to find, when she finally pushed through the crowd, that a young man with Down's syndrome was already seated at it.

Making no effort to conceal her exasperation at this turn of events, she stacked her heavy parcels around the other chair, removed her overcoat, sat down and finally opened a packet of biscuits on the table. Each time she reached for a biscuit, her unwelcome but smiling companion reached for one too.

This impertinence was too much for the woman. Not wishing to make a scene, but inwardly raging, she gulped down her tea, and reached for her belongings and her coat. As she got to her feet, her packet of biscuits, lying hidden in her ample lap, rolled gently to the floor.

One of the reasons given for our negativity towards those who have disabilities is that they remind us of all that is 'not normal' within ourselves, all that is 'different', all that we interpret as ill or unacceptable. In his beautiful *The Road to Daybreak*, Henri Nouwen offers an insight painfully gained during the year he spent at L'Arche, in France, a community devoted to the care of vulnerable people with learning difficulties.

'Often they are capable of unmasking our own impatience, irritation, jealousy, thus making us honest with ourselves. For them what matters is a true relationship, a real friendship, a faithful presence. Many mentally handicapped people experience themselves as a disappointment to their parents, a burden to their families, a nuisance to their friends,' wrote Nouwen. 'Their hearts, never sure of their worth, register with extreme sensitivity what is real care and what is false, what is true affection and what are empty words. Thus they often reveal to us our own hypocrisies.'

The whole point of the Incarnation, and of every moment of the life of Jesus, is to reveal that such people are, in fact, our spiritual teachers. Jean Vanier, the spiritual giant and champion of the *anawim* – the disabled, the poor, the marginalised, the alienated – of our times wrote: 'In some way their anguish awakened my own anguish, their poverty my own poverty. This is an incredible discovery … that the Good News is announced to the poor, not to those who serve them. Our acceptance of handicapped people as they are, with all their disabilities, weaknesses and frailties, teaches us to accept every human being, and ourselves, to accept the fundamental wound inside …'

How do they teach us? Here are a few very personal memories. My brother Joseph had Down's syndrome. He lived at home all his life. And during the most difficult times, especially when Joseph's severe diabetes demanded unrelenting attention, my mother was sustained by her belief that in caring for Joseph she was entertaining angels.

Many decades ago, I asked her to write a few things about her life with Joseph. She recounted the depth of her pain. She glossed over nothing. The whole family was intrinsically caught up in the mess and mystery of it all. There was nothing romantic in her letter. But in her eyes, Joseph was utterly beautiful. Her life, she wrote, was 'crammed with blessings'.

She recalled how he loved to celebrate, to play, to break every negotiable regulation. He faithfully followed Meister Eckhart's recommendation 'to live without a why'. He had his own timing – the timing of the present moment. He forgave even as he breathed. He carried no resentment; nor could he remember our recent impatience with him, our irritation, our petty complaining. On a good day, his presence was healing; his grace tangible.

'Joseph was in Killarney one day, with Maura, his sister,' my mother had written, 'and there was a street fiddler playing merrily at the corner. The man's cap was on the ground waiting for the money from the passers-by. Joseph indicated to Maura his need for a coin (he never *owned* anything, or carried anything in his pockets). But he did not think it was right to throw the 20p into the cap, so he handed it, instead, to the music man who appreciated Joseph's gesture of recognising his dignity. He stopped playing to smile and shake Joseph's hand.'

Joseph and his friends had a deep sense of the sacred. They carried a special awareness of the holy. They loved the songs, the ritual, the lights, the whole atmosphere of their beloved 'Faith and Light Masses'. With the utmost reverence they would receive Holy Communion. Their minds knew nothing about transubstantiation or consubstantiality, but their hearts knew how to adore.

Joseph never spoke a normal word. What really upset me, as I read my mother's words again, was my memory of Joseph's frustration, almost despair, when he could not figure out what we were talking about, laughing about or getting excited about at our meals at home. We tend to forget their inner pain. Any form of rejection is a knife through the souls of people like Joseph.

My mother wrote that Joseph knew little about conformity or social expectations. To live with him, you had to loosen up, lighten up, let go of all pretensions to grandeur. Impervious to class, he saw everyone as equal. At home as he was with visiting bishops, the sight of a crying baby, a bandaged head or any sign of human distress commanded his full and loving attention. She noted that despite the term 'handicapped', he was the most gracious and free spirit of all of us. Nobody taught Joseph how to dance.

Towards the end of Morris West's *The Clowns of God*, there is a poignant scene where some doubtful but well-intentioned people are asking God for a sign – to heal a girl in their community who has learning disabilities. God replies: 'I could do it; but I will not. I gave this mite a gift I denied to all of you – eternal innocence. To you she looks imperfect, but to me she is flawless, like the bud that dies unopened … She will never destroy. The little one is my sign to you. Treasure her.'

While the Leaves Fall

As Autumn takes hold, the mood, the traditions, even the weather of the month of November often turn our thoughts to those whom we have lost. But death need not mean the loss of meaning – love and loss are for ever inextricably linked.

November winds carry echoes of loss. It is the month of All Saints and All Souls, when memories that bless and burn come back to haunt us. We sense anew the absence of the loves of our lives. But by now we have learnt that love and loss go together. If you love, you are sure to suffer; if you do not love, you will suffer even more.

Most of us, in fact, in the fine resiliency of the human soul, are willing to try loving, again and again, though we understand how vulnerable that makes us to loss. But we cannot live without love and loss. They are written into our DNA; into the very nature of life itself.

One way or another, loss forever shadows the light of our lives. And the more we love people and things, and the more attached we are to our dreams and hopes, the more deeply we will feel their loss. Each of us has our own story of loves and losses, of coping with the raw joys and hurting edges they score into our soul.

The impact of loss is often unpredictable, and can be utterly poignant. It can suddenly ambush you, that aching sense of someone's absence brought on by a spring morning, a summer pathway, an autumn sky, an empty chair, the first Christmas carol you must listen to alone.

Long after she had died, the sight of some scribbled comments by my mother, tucked away in the pages of the book I was rereading, twisted my heart in a way impossible to describe. Loving someone wraps invisible blankets of blessing around both people. The most beautiful and essential parts of us are entwined with those of the other. These invisible realities are often below consciousness.

I remember a mother in my last parish telling me that she suddenly woke up one night with the shocking realisation that her son had just died. This awareness came to her, I felt, not as any kind of sad news from the outside, so to speak: it came from within, a sense of the absence of an invisible bonding that was central to the throbbing substance of both their lives. It was not the arrival of something new that had come into her head; it was the death of something essential that had left her heart.

Spiritual writer Henri Nouwen reflected on the inescapable presence of loss. 'There is a quality of sadness that pervades all the moments of life. It seems that there is no such thing as clearcut pure joy; even in the happiest times we sense a tinge of loss … But this intimate experience of loss can point beyond the limits of our existence.'

When our hearts are broken from bitter mourning, there is little comfort in Nouwen's words. Our mourning is not turned into dancing overnight. We can discern no hidden grace in grief and loss. We are like a seed buried in the darkness, alone and waiting.

It is only when the time is right, when the heart is ready, that loss, like a midwife, brings something very special and undreamt of into the emptiness of our lives. The moment of a new and slowly emerging reality will only come when we trust the possibility of such a resurrection, and open ourselves to it.

Our life, we discover, has not lost its meaning. Something in our soul forever senses possibility. In 'Love without Frontiers', Preston-born poet Phoebe Hesketh wrote:

> *A love without frontiers that sees without eyes,*
> *Is present in absence and never denies*
> *The unexplored country beyond.*[20]

Loss is like a teacher. Its value lies in the space it makes for something new to grow. 'Loss makes vital clearance in the soul,' wrote John O'Donohue. 'Loss is the sister of discovery; it is vital to openness; though it certainly brings much pain.' Where the loss is caused by the death of a dearly-loved friend or relation, that sense of loss may now begin to open the slow door to another way of being with that person. Unrestricted by time and place, a new intimacy becomes possible. Jesus was so conscious of that mysterious transition – the need to leave us so as to possess us more intimately.

The felt sting of death lessens; the reality of the love does not. No matter what subsequently happens, where love was once true, it will never be replaced. Part of you will always be a presence around the other, and from their unseen places, they will most certainly be minding us with the purest love.

This is the message of the angel of grief. We do not have to become stuck for ever in the sands of sorrow. We step free beyond it. There is a wider and firmer space in which to move with the rhythm of life. It does not mean that we turn away from the person or place that we no longer experience as we once did. Nor does it mean that a new love replaces the old one. True love is not like that.

In *The Unfilled Gap*, theologian Dietrich Bonhoeffer wrote about the dynamic of space between those who have truly loved: 'Nothing can fill the gap when we are away from those we love, and it would be wrong to try to find anything, since leaving the gap unfilled preserves the bond between us. It is nonsense to say that God fills the gap. He does not fill it but keeps it empty, so that communion with another may be kept alive even at the cost of pain.'

There is a nourishing paradox in the way another peerless theologian, Karl Rahner, reflects on the unfilled gap. 'There is no such thing in either the world or the heart as a vacuum,' he said. 'And wherever space is really left by death, by renunciation, by parting, by apparent emptiness, provided that the emptiness is not filled by the world, or activity, or noise, or the deadly grief of the world – there is God.'

Those who have loved and lost, and grown through it all, have already tasted death and resurrection. They have followed their passion, they have risked for love; they have been devastated by loss. And because they loved and trusted life once, the final death will never be a fearful stranger.

Sense of Heaven

As the drives and energies of life's morning slip away with the coming of the afternoon, one realises that to be honest and transparent is more important than to be successful or respected; that it is more blessed to be truly human and spiritual than religious or clerical.

Moved recently by the brooding presence of autumn, I revisited Richmond Park in south-west London, where I used to jog daily when I worked at St Mary's University College, Twickenham. As I made my way from gate to gate – Roehampton, Richmond, Kingston, Robin Hood – the memories came crowding in with unexpected clarity.

I walked around it twice. The first time I reflected on the first half of my life; the second time on my journey since. I was at full stretch in those early years. Nothing was too much to do, no challenge too difficult, no mountain too high.

I said 'yes' to everything. Upwardly mobile and ambitious, I did further studies in theology, learning how to write, how to teach (if such gifts can ever be learned). These were decades of hard graft, of traumas and anxieties, of successes and excesses. There was much plotting, planning and persuading, many aspirations and failures, all the necessary pre-midlife experiences.

It was during the first half of my life that I was sent by the bishop to the newly-opened Corpus Christi College in Notting Hill Gate, west London. That was a year of wonder – maybe more delighted shock than wonder. The veils were parted there, the doors flung open, the imagination set free.

Vatican II had just brought an astonishing and life-giving summer into our lives. A new passion for the possible was firing us up as we listened to the visiting prophets of that time. God's love was unconditional. The Church was the protecting mother of Jesus' dream for the world.

Liturgy was the purifying celebration of the divinity of our daily lives. Catechesis was about liberating our hearts for miracles. Contemplation was the moment of intimacy between lovers. Our imagination and senses were angels of grace. And we moved to the rhythms of the Incarnation.

Before it reached its tenth birthday, on a winter's day, the college door was suddenly locked. Looking back now, I wonder if we lock out too many voices – those of the Vatican Council, of our best theologians, of the poor, of the earth and of women – all prophets of our salvation. Why does the first Crucifixion still go on?

During the second half of my life, I am learning to grow by subtraction. These are the decades of the inner work. We move into another place, the afternoon of our life, which cannot be lived by the drives and energies of life's morning. 'What is a normal goal to a young person, becomes a neurotic hindrance in old age,' wrote Carl Jung.

At this time of life, one learns that to be transparent and honest is more important than to be successful or respected; that it is more blessed to be truly human and spiritual than religious or clerical. 'When we are only victorious over small things, it leaves us feeling small,' wrote Rainer Maria Rilke.

I'm learning that one can become old without becoming aged. Libby Purves wrote recently about an aged agelessness. 'There can be a sort of lightness, a sense of having seen and suffered much, but accepting that you can be rich in what you have lost.'

Bette Davis reminded us that 'old age is not for sissies'. She was right. Without a certain discipline and purpose of mind, the shadows of bitterness, cynicism or despair can easily begin their deadly work in us. We are right to be concerned about poverty and pensions, about dementia and care. But we must also, from time to time, sit back in wonder at our lives, savour the flavour of many graced experiences, of those unexpected moments of love that still fill us with gratitude and hope.

Part of that wonder, for me, is the reassurance that the complexities of my life are not mine alone; that in spite of peculiarities, extremes and failures, I am no different from others in their eccentricities, pathological desires and secrets. I am not out of step with other normal human beings, walking around inside their own human skin. Everyone is wounded; everyone is hurting; everyone is imperfect. All are sinners.

'The Scriptures are filled with stories of people close to God, even as their own lives are often fraught with mess, confusion, frustration, betrayal, infidelity and sin,' writer and theologian Ronald Rolheiser reminds us. 'There are no simple human beings, immune to the psychological, sexual and relational complexities that beset us all.'

Also, during these later years, if we are lucky, a clearer self-awareness of our place in the grand scheme of things may be revealed. After many decades, a pattern of our consistent contribution emerges, the abiding melody that runs through the mix and mess and mystery of our life's decisions and choices.

Blessed John Henry Newman wrote about the importance of being able, one day, to name and nourish that incarnate gift, that enduring song, entrusted to us – and to nobody else.

Irish novelist Colm Tóibin recently wrote about his transition into the second half of life. He does not think at all about his many literary achievements. But he does reflect on the parable of the talents. 'I think I was given one talent,' he wrote, 'as minor as it may be, and I just work hard at it and try to be as truthful to it as I possibly can.'

The gradual harvesting of our lives brings many revelations. I have noticed, for instance, how often our pet beliefs, our commitment to rules and rubrics, to this or that certainty, seem to lose their influence over us. This usually happens when we finally surrender to the embrace of a God who is utterly different from anything we ever imagined. Once you have experienced even a hint of such a beautiful lover, there is no going back.

In his *Confessions*, St Augustine wrote: 'You were within, but I was without. You were with me but I was not with you. So you called, you shouted, you broke my deafness, you flared, blazed, and banished my blindness. You lavished your fragrance – and I gasped.'

These contemplative years, then, are never meant to be a slow and slumbering slide into terminal places. They may, in fact, contain epiphanies of a vital presence, when we hold ourselves still, 'quivering with each moment', as the mystic Rumi wrote, 'like a drop of mercury'. Such vibrant attentiveness, uniquely in later life, is what the mystics call 'the sense of heaven'.

Brightest Presence in the Darkest Places

Liturgy for its own sake is always a danger for the Church, leading to a ritualism that can deter people from belonging to it. It is now time for the Church to renew its public way of worship and root it in all the mess, misery and riches of people's lives.

'Give me one good reason for going back to the sacraments.' Priests are often faced with this question by those quitting the liturgical life of the Church. Such disaffected Catholics get tired of the relentless catechism of warnings and the litanies of instructions, but perhaps most of all the irrelevance of Sunday worship to their difficult lives. That irrelevance is the tipping point for many disillusioned Catholics today.

Professor John Baldovin SJ, in his acclaimed *Reforming the Liturgy* (2009), reminds us that liturgy must never separate the sacred from the profane. 'Giving attention to the liturgy for the liturgy's sake alone, as an end in itself,' he said, 'is not Christian faith: it is narcissistic obsession.'[21] The revered liturgical pioneer Fr James Crichton referred to it as 'the meaningless performance called ritualism'.

In *Porta Fidei* (2011), the apostolic letter, Pope Emeritus Benedict saw the 'Year of Faith' as 'a good opportunity to intensify the celebration of the faith in the liturgy and the Eucharist'. But the liturgy, at the moment, has lost its way, having drifted from its secure anchor in the human condition, the Word made flesh. The recent imposition of the 'new translation', the lifting of restrictions on the Extraordinary Form of the Mass, the relentless and subtle pressure to return to the liturgical mentality and practice of the past, are all affecting the faith of God's people. How can a peaceful balance be restored to this graceless running battle that the liturgy has become?

For a start we need to look again at the spirit of Vatican II's *Sacrosanctum Concilium*. 'The liturgy', it states, 'sanctifies almost every event in (people's) lives (*SC* 61).' Weekly worship is the Incarnation made tangible for God's needy people, it states. Parishioners want to experience God in the middle of the mess and mystery of each day. Liturgy has, you might say, become too heavenly to be of any earthly use. When a more life-centred, incarnational and truly traditional theology of liturgy is unpacked for parishioners, a radical shift in how they understand the sacraments will follow.

Liturgical celebration is not about inviting God into the 'secular' lives of parishioners. Nor is it about inviting parishioners' 'secular' lives into the holiness of the Church on a Sunday morning. Rather it is the sublime ritual for making explicit what is already and always at the heart of our loves, our lives and our pain, thus healing and encouraging us, revealing to us that God's brightest presence is hidden in our darkest places. There is nothing in life so scientific, so secular or so sinful, as St Paul points out, that we cannot find God in it.

This seriously neglected understanding of liturgy urgently needs to be restored. It breathes again in the English and Welsh Bishops' Conference study *On the Way to Life* (2005). The Jesuit authors, basing their work on the implications of the Incarnation, emphasise that, 'The theology of nature and grace that informs Vatican II recovers "the ordinary" as the place of grace; hence holiness is not something exceptional ... The liturgy celebrates our embodiedness.'

The unacknowledged assumption still is that it is primarily to the liturgy that we must look for the experience of the sacred. But this is not a truly incarnational belief. 'Liturgical celebration', observes theologian Richard McBrien, 'does not cause grace in the sense that grace is otherwise unavailable. The offer of grace is already present to the world in God's original self-giving. The sacraments signify, celebrate and draw out of us, what God is, in a sense, already doing everywhere and for all.'

The theologian Karl Rahner reminds us that sacraments must be seen as manifestations of that grace, which is at work everywhere in human history where women and men are getting on with their lives in everyday ways. A real understanding of the Eucharist, he holds, reveals the milieu of that mysterious grace which governs our whole life – 'the grace that finds its victory in the monotony, pain and ordinariness of daily life'.

Another perspective may help to clarify these reflections. Rahner has often written about a sacramentality of humanity – a 'liturgy of the world' as well as a 'liturgy of the Church'. He sees the progress of the human story and the evolving universe as a liturgy of human life. By this he means that the material world itself, and our place in it, are already an intimate dimension of the glory of God.

The liturgy of the Church, then, gives explicit and dramatic expression to the liturgy of the world, to the hidden holiness of what seems 'ordinary'; it completes, purifies, celebrates and intensifies it. Without the liturgy of the Church, we would not be able to grasp fully the astonishing height and depth, the love and meaning of the daily liturgy of the world, first revealed in the mystery of the Incarnation.

We have difficulty recognising the holy liturgy of our lived lives in the world, not because it occurs so rarely, but because it occurs so often. That is why the real world must forever be at the centre of our liturgical celebration. Without honouring the authentic lives and experiences of people, the raw reality of their emotions, our Sunday liturgy will betray the radical revelation of the Incarnation.

We gather for Sunday worship not because our secular lives are empty of divinity, but because we need to honour all the grace-filled moments already trembling in those same human lives, often dark and hidden in our hurting hearts, sometimes shining like hope in our eyes. Church liturgy has the same hopes and goals and dreams for each human heart as Jesus had when he walked among us. The experience in church of true, life-nourishing liturgy will bring home to wavering Mass-goers the tangible implications of Incarnation –

that the presence of God is in their efforts to stay in love, in the families they struggle to hold together, in their terrible anxiety about money and mortgages, in their fears for their health, in their depressions and temptations, in their despair before a world in pain, in their loss of faith, in all their experiences of death and hope and in their desire to worship God.

Will reflections such as these cut any ice with the disillusioned faithful departing our churches, with those who say 'Give me one good reason for going back to the sacraments'?

Unblocking the Light

For the Lenten pilgrim, the most difficult aspect of the journey to Easter involves a purging of the ego and an inward transparency. It is an extraordinary challenge but one that is life-transforming.

A touching film made in 2004 is quietly doing the rounds again. It's called *As it is in Heaven*. Middle-aged Daniel is a famous musician who is stressed because of the intensity of his workload. He takes a sabbatical back to his childhood village in the Netherlands. The locals enlist his reluctant help with the very mediocre church choir.

'The music is there,' he told them. 'It is all around us. All we have to do is "take it down".' They do not understand him. He tries to explain that they will never succeed in allowing that true, pure sound to emerge and fill them, until they themselves are open enough, and empty enough, to trust and receive it. Much of the film is about the long, hard struggle of the singers to find the courage and inner freedom without which they will never find their own real voice.

Grace, too, is all around us. Like music, as Mozart said, it fills the world. But until we become inwardly transparent there will be no true transformation. This is the real challenge and discipline of the spiritual life. Because we are blocked within, we cannot 'take it down'. Once opened, the miracle follows. It has to follow. It is the nature of grace and the grace of our nature to do so.

Spiritual writers suggest horizons by which to set our compass for the inner journey to the authentic self. A well-travelled route of the saints is the way of surrender. It is the relinquishing of control, the unseating of the proud ego. Even for the holiest of souls, this is almost impossible to do. Suffering has been described as that state when, for whatever reason, we no longer have control over our lives or our future.

We are terrified, for instance, when our health is beyond healing, when a love is beyond rekindling, when a damage done is irreparable, when our good name is irretrievably lost. To surrender, we fear, is to lose our sense of self, our self-sufficiency, our sense of worthiness – to become unbearably at the mercy of others.

'If we take our vulnerable shell to be our true identity, if we think our mask is our true face, we will protect it with fabrications even at the cost of violating our own truth,' wrote Thomas Merton. We will never 'take down' the grace. To purify our own ever-blessed essence is the reason for all our traditional Lenten practices of repentance, self-denial, almsgiving and prayer. Otherwise the elemental human split and stain within us only darkens more.

In spite of our fallenness, what we are all unceasingly searching for is someone to surrender to, someone in whom we can define ourselves. 'God', writes Richard Rohr, 'is the only one we can surrender to without losing ourselves.' The irony is that we actually and finally do find ourselves, but now in a whole new and much larger field of meaning.

Once we let go of our need to control, to be independent; once we allow the utterly transforming love of God to invade the deepest levels of our complicated souls, then we notice that we are moving to another place where many things begin to matter much less to us, and a few things begin to matter much more.

Another classic and connected counsel for serious Lenten pilgrims is a commitment to a painful *metanoia*, to a radical self-purification. We slowly begin to notice that fear and resentment block the nourishing light from restoring our souls. We start to realise that these negative, diminishing emotions are, in the words of the Ash Wednesday readings, 'corroding the spirit'. This kind of dawning readiness and openness, with its guaranteed harvest of graces, is beyond the capacity of what St Thomas Aquinas called the *anima pusilla* – the small self, the false soul. Lent is a blessed season to discover the *anima magna* within us, the large soul. So many trappings of religion fall away at that most revealing moment, when we discover that beautiful soul, when we choose it, and decide to live it into our destiny. That is when the grace notes ring in our heart.

This moment has been described as the most courageous act of our lives; the personal passover for which we were born. But there is nothing automatic about it. Spiritual maturity nearly always emerges only from the experiences of futility, fall or failure. At such times, as we try to breathe into the fearful pain, we may hear an inner invitation into a deeply desired freedom. Our 'yes' to that invitation will play havoc with our daily routines, with the reign of the ego, and with our religious pretensions. It will make us think and feel about our faith in a way we never did before. It will purify and clarify our understanding of the Church, and a new, tender and demanding insight into the Gospel of Jesus will captivate our hearts.

A final challenge to the soul is to discern the excessiveness in our lives – our congenital drive towards acquiring more, often in a mindless kind of greed. Fr Ronald Rolheiser writes: 'When excess enters, enjoyment departs, as does freedom. Compulsion sets in. Now we begin to seek a thing, not because it will bring us joy, but because we are driven to have it. Excess is a substitute for enjoyment.'

The story goes that Joseph Heller, author of *Catch 22*, was once told about a fund manager who made more money that very day than he did from all his books combined. Heller replied, 'Then I have something he will never have. Enough.' Spiritual writer Mary Jo Leddy insists that at some point in Lent we must say, mean and live the following; 'It's enough. I have enough. I am enough. Life is enough. With all my heart I thank you.'

When it comes to personal authenticity and transparency, there are no shortcuts, no cheap graces. Inner purity of heart has to be hewn out of the rocks of our resistance. Even for Jesus, the Human One, there was a terrible darkness during his forty desert days. And there were cups of pain he gagged on. Being overwhelmed by God is a terrible experience.

'An encounter with the divine', a mystic-friend of mine recently wrote, 'is not a gentle affair, filled with flowers and chirping birds. It is like being woken up by an earthquake. It shakes us to the very core of our being, crushes our pretence. God topples the false temples of our lives.'

Emily Dickinson puts it this way:

> *He stuns you by Degrees –*
> *Prepares your brittle nature*
> *For the etherial Blow …*
> *Then nearer – Then so – slow –*
>
> *Your Breath – has time to straighten –*
> *Your Brain – to bubble cool –*
> *Deals One – imperial thunderbolt –*
> *That scalps your naked soul.*[22]

And did those Feet ...

Dancing is most usually seen as exuberant and joyful, but it articulates the entire spectrum of human emotions, encompassing everything from freedom to deepest loss and death itself.

The Celtic harvest festival *Lughnasadh* on 1 August takes its name from the Irish god Lugh. It has been celebrated until recently at wakes, fairs and summer revels in Wales, Scotland, the Isle of Man and Ireland. Dancers would whirl around an effigy of the harvest goddess, touching her garlands or snatching a ribbon from her hair to ensure fruitful, fertile fields for the next year.

This feast is the backdrop chosen by Irish playwright Brian Friel as the setting for his beautiful play *Dancing at Lughnasa*. It features five sisters in their County Donegal cottage in 1936. Things are not good for them. Disgrace, penury and a great sadness are stifling their souls.

At the end of the play, in a most extraordinary burst of combined energy, the women release their profound emotional suppression. Their celebrated dance gives a glimpse of the unquenchable passions that come from far beyond words, far beyond the sisters' kitchen window. Some kind of sacramental shutter was thrown open and, for a moment, unbidden, a suppressed wildness, desperation even, burst free from the shadows of their souls. It ended with a terrible stillness.

We dance in our distress. We dance to survive. The American poet Mary Oliver once encountered an old man in 'a headdress of feathers' who 'danced in a kind of surly rapture'. In 'Two Kinds of Deliverance' she writes:

> *As for the pain*
> *of others, of course it tries to be*
> *abstract, but then*
>
> *there flares up out of a vanished wilderness, like fire,*
> *still blistering: the wrinkled face*
> *of an old Chippewa*
> *smiling, hating us,*
> *dancing for his life.*[23]

People dance for many reasons. We dance our joy, our freedom, our worship, our deepest loss. Recently, on an empty day, I went to see *Billy Elliot* again. At the end of his disastrous interview at the Royal School of Ballet, he was given a last chance. They asked him what he felt when he danced. 'It sort of feels good,' he said. 'It starts stiff and that, but once I get going then I – like – forget everything and sort of disappear. Like I feel a change in my whole body. There's fire in me. I'm just there, flyin' like a bird, like electricity, yeah, like electricity.'

'When grace enters,' wrote W. H. Auden, 'humans must dance.' And when does grace enter? It enters, when, for instance, I make the choice each morning to live freely today rather than exist like a victim, to run the way of beauty rather than stumble along the blind way. When I begin to believe that God is always holding on to me, no matter what – I want to dance.

A kairos time and timing for dancing is when we begin, after many years, to live our unlived lives, so as to die without regret. We create a tiny dance floor when we hold off, even for a split second, these dark and deadly thoughts, allowing our souls a sliver of saving light. We can dance in that space because in it we have regained our blessed balance, our divine energy. This space may last the length of a human breath, but it hides and reveals the heart of redemption.

Something in all of us wants to dance when courage taps us on the shoulder, when the chains of fear and the baggage of false guilt fall from our shoulders. We want to dance when we hear the music of hope. And sometimes we dance when there's no alternative. An eighty-three-year-old woman once said: 'Life may not be the party we hoped for, but while we are here, we might as well dance.'

The time to dance is now. Too often we think that it is only when our worries are over, our health is restored, our job is secure, the bills are paid, our relationships are back on track, our mind is at peace and our corns are pared that we can rejoice and dance. But we cannot put our lives on hold and wait for the perfect space and moment for dancing. Tomorrow is not always our dancing day.

The urge to dance and the urge to despair may be partners on the floor of our souls. Theologian Leonardo Boff believed that without our darkness as well as our light, our demons as well as our angels, our hearts will never truly dance. Writer Fr John Shea believes that: 'Life will always include suffering. When we spend all our energies in rejoicing only in those parts of our days that are painless, we will never enter into the dance of life because of too many unreal expectations.'

There is no energy left for dancing when we are not living the life we love, but rather the life expected of us. 'We have fallen out of rhythm with the secret signature and light of our own nature,' is how John O'Donohue puts it. 'We need to feel the soul's dream with the wonder of a child approaching a threshold of discovery. We come into rhythm with ourselves, and then gradually learn to dance beautifully on this magnificent earth.'

Albert Einstein holds that everything dances. 'Human beings, vegetables and cosmic dust', he wrote, 'all dance to a mysterious tune intoned in the distance by an invisible player.' That invisible player is God. The early Church Fathers used the word *perichoresis* to describe the gracious movement of mutuality between the persons of the Blessed Trinity in each person's soul. Richard Rohr calls it 'God's circle-dance of communion'.

That dancing Trinity is within us all, beckoning us to join in. The invitation is echoed by Ronan Keating of Boyzone when he sings:

Promise me that you'll give faith a fighting chance;
And when you get the chance to sit it out or dance,
— I hope you dance.

Treasured beyond Measure

Too often at Christmas, the real magic is missed.
There is nothing infantile about the infant;
the innocence of the child is the power of God filling the hearts
and souls of all beloved and broken people with hope and light.

Back in the 1950s, during December days, at around 6 p.m., a small army of boys and girls were collected from the neighbouring villages of Knocknagree, Gneeveguilla and Barraduff, and taken to Rathmore Creamery, for the killing and plucking of the Christmas turkeys and geese. The staff did the killing; we did the plucking.

It was pure torture. Plucking resistant pin feathers from a tough and bony old bird was hardly an inspiring Advent ritual. It was ninepence for a cock, sixpence for a hen. The hens were easy. I wasted my whole first night trying to pluck a cock. Again and again I was refused my money – either there were some impossible feathers still attached, or the skin was bruised or bleeding, or the plucking checker did not like me.

This was my first introduction to paid work. Looking back now, I remember how upset I was at that hard world of earning, meriting and competing. There was little generosity in that smelly shed of flying fleas and feathers. You had to cajole and bargain for every last penny at the payout table. Even in those young years, I wanted another kind of world – a more forgiving one, a more loving one, where all the pin feathers do not have to be removed. With a child's clarity, I longed for things to be different. I discovered later that they already were. But nobody told us.

One day, if we are lucky, the impact of Christmas stuns us. Something remarkable begins to dawn on us – the recognition that, despite its ugliness and evil, this wounded world is alive with love. We are treasured beyond measure by a mercy that does not depend on our worthiness – that carries no inspection for perfection.

Every year, we have Advent to remember and delight in this transforming story, this radical revelation that the divine Mystery is now flesh of our flesh, as intimate as our senses. The mystic within us knows that the same holds true of the world itself, that we must cherish it, because now we know it to be the precious body of God.

Incarnation is about the way we see things, the way we get hints of the holy, hidden nature of everything, especially of the experiences of our lives. Think, for instance, of the most complete, loving moment you can remember. Think of all that has ever moved you profoundly, whether this be the silence of the darkness, the forgiveness of a friend, or the wind in the winter trees. All of that is unearned, undeserved. And it is all free. We know this because of the baby.

There will, of course, be days when we doubt this. There is too much confusion around us, too much pain inside us. We lose our longing for the light. One Sunday at Mass we prayed for the removal of 'the darkness that blinds us to the vision that fills the mind.' Midnight Mass reveals, to those who have learnt to see, that these beautiful prayers are already answered – every day.

Reflect, for instance, on the utter surprise of feeling the invincible Spirit move in you, of sensing there is nothing you cannot be, or do. Think of the most liberating moments in your life – when, for instance, at the end of your worst night of loss, you still got up, drew back the curtains, and, without knowing why, your stalled heart began to beat with hope again.

Or think of the most courageous moment that still makes your eyes shine. Think of the time when you reached way beyond yourself, when you stretched for what was out of reach, when someone or something carried you to a place you had only dreamed of, when you felt at one with everything, and sensed that your forgiving look was a small sacrament of universal peace.

Remember the sublime music that moved you to tears, the dance that made you throw back your head and laugh out loud, the painting that touched your hidden passion, the possibility or the person that stole your heart. That is when you were experiencing the excitement we call God, revealed first in the small lover on straw who smiled at the star above him, and cried at the cross he glimpsed beneath it.

Too often, at Christmas, we perennially miss the real magic – that in his subsequent death and Resurrection, the 'baby Jesus' is, in fact, revealed to be the Cosmic Christ who flattens the hills of injustice and fills the valleys with hope, the heart, soul and saviour of God's beloved and broken people, the mighty 'firstborn of all Creation', the pulsing being of all that lives. There is nothing infantile about the infant. Christmas is already Easter.

We look at the baby and sight trembles into insight, seeing is transformed by recognition. Advent grace is for attuning the senses of the soul to the rhythm of God's heart in every heartbeat. The poets know this. Gerard Manley Hopkins reminds us of 'the face behind the face', Kathleen Raine of 'the mountain behind the mountain', Seamus Heaney of 'the horizon behind the horizon' and St Paul of 'the energy behind all energies'. That's the revealing language of the traditional 'catholic imagination'.

'The day of my spiritual awakening', wrote Rhineland mystic Mechtild of Magdeburg, 'was the day I saw – and knew I saw – all things in God and God in all things.' Incarnation is about recognising divine beauty – usually in deep disguise. Can you think of a time when you saw into the heart of a gesture, a passing event, any sensation – really and truly saw into it, through the lens of Christmas?

In 'Snow Geese', poet Mary Oliver tells of her sacramental glimpse into the mystery of the ordinary:

> *One fall day I heard*
> *above me, and above the sting of the wind, a sound*
> *I did not know, and my look shot upward; it was*

a flock of snow geese, winging it
*   faster than the ones we usually see,*
and, being the color of snow, catching the sun

so they were, in part at least, golden ...

I have never
seen them again.

Maybe I will, someday, somewhere.
Maybe I won't.
It doesn't matter.
What matters
is that, when I saw them,
I saw them
as through the veil, secretly, joyfully, clearly.[24]

God needs your Body to Dance

We can journey from frailty to freedom in our lives, and that progress is made, necessarily, not only in the mind but also in the body. To reach this goal, like the best dancers, we must 'swallow fire'.

'A flamenco dancer, lurking under the shadow, prepared for the terror of her dance. Somebody has wounded her in words, alluding to the fact that she had no fire or duende. She knows she has to dance her way past her limitations, and that this may destroy her forever …

'When the music starts she begins her dance, with ritual slowness. Then she stamps out the dampness from her soul. Then she stamps fire into her loins. She takes on a strange enchanted glow. With a dark tragic rage, shouting, she hurls her hungers, her doubts, her terrors and her secular prayer for more light into the spaces around her. Soon she becomes a wild unknown force, glowing in her death, dancing from her wound, dying in her dance.'

Ben Okri wrote this story about the power of transcendence. It takes courage to dance, he said. This was the dance into another place. The dancer's body carried her from frailty to freedom. While she danced she was taken beyond herself, to the destined space she was made to move in. 'We seldom try', wrote Okri, 'for that beautiful greatness brooding in the mystery of our body and blood.'[25]

Christmas is the feast of the body: it celebrates the flesh. Yet too often we are taught to distrust the beauty and wisdom of the body. But they are the Sacrament of the Incarnation. Redemption, Resurrection, the abundant life – they are ever only real when experienced in our essential humanity. It is in our bodies that we experience heaven. And in them that God experiences earth. Tradition calls this 'the dance of the Hypostatic Union in the Human One'.

> *And God said:*
> *May you delight in your body.*
> *It is my body too.*
> *Don't you know you are my senses?*
> *Without your body I cannot be.*

Were we to believe even a whisper of that revelation, adults would gather around the Christmas crib with astonished faces – astonished, as if for the first time, at the promised possibilities for their bodies and for the body of the world. It is a blessed scene about our own infancy and destiny as well as that of Jesus – a graced infancy in a graced humanity that grows perfectly human even after our death, in the youthfulness of heaven. But not without its necessary deprivations and tears.

Indeed, after the Resurrection, the physical wounds of Jesus are ever honoured. Embodiment, even in its pain and fragility, seems to be an essential condition of divinity. Michael Symmons Roberts writes in 'Food for Risen Bodies II':

> *Now on Tiberias' shores he grills*
> *a carp and catfish breakfast on a charcoal fire.*
> *This is not hunger, is resurrection:*
>
> *he eats because he can, and wants to*
> *taste the scales, the moist flakes of the sea,*
> *to rub the salt into his wounds.*[26]

Christmas reveals that we are all born with a divine star. Our bodies carry auras of inner loveliness. That is the meaning of the hallowed halo around the baby's sleepy head. We all have one! Its brightness does not depend on being successful at religion, on acquiring virtues and overcoming vices, on enforced beliefs and passing worthiness tests.

In 'Icon', Lynn Roberts writes of an ordinary, hard-working woman. The poem ends:

> Her face is olive and her hands have pads
> of calloused skin from grinding grain for flour;
> but if you concentrate, you'll see, perhaps,
> through her chemise a faint transparency
> which glows – as though she's swallowed fire.[27]

'As though she's swallowed fire' – like the flamenco dancer in her wild catharsis, like all our bodies when they fall in love with the God within them. That's the evocative language that best expresses the assumption of a receptive humanity by a hopelessly smitten divinity. 'As though she's swallowed fire' – not even the angels could say those words. Only we, who have senses.

In a delightful Advent homily one thousand years ago, St Symeon wrote so beautifully of a lambent healing in our vulnerable bodies:

> We awaken in Christ's body
> as Christ awakens our bodies ...
>
> and everything that is hurt, everything
> that seemed to us ...
> maimed, ugly, irreparably
> damaged, is in Him transformed
> and recognized as whole, as lovely,
> and radiant in His light.[28]

There is a shocking intensity about God's initial and passionate desire to possess us. At the beginning, when shaping Adam and Eve out of the new mud, God was carefully forming all our human bodies as we know and experience them, as God-made-tangible, enjoyable and lovable. And that first desire was never thwarted. Original sin is the strange resistance we carry to believing such good news.

Without the baby in the midnight crib, we would simply forget, as Richard Rohr OFM puts it, that our very DNA is divine. That DNA does not belong only to a chosen race, a people set apart. It belongs to everyone.

Christmas, therefore, asks us to name and recognise our own issues and prejudices with the human body in all its peculiarities, in its particular sexuality and ambiguity. It urges us to value and to embrace all those we recklessly label, scapegoat and sinfully diminish in our graceless ignorance and fear.

To raise our hands at anyone in our own home, to physically or spiritually abuse a child, to torture or mutilate anyone, for any reason, is to strike out at God's own face. So we learn to respect and grant justice to one another as divinely embodied people, with all our emotional differences. The crib confronts us with another way of understanding what incarnate beauty looks like. Incarnation irrevocably reveals that God has carefully created and tenderly blessed all people with dignity and worthiness. It insists that the first places at the holy altar of equality are always reserved for such special and beloved children of God.

Joseph, my brother, who had Down's syndrome (and who was once deemed unworthy to take his place at that table to make his First Holy Communion), loved dancing. Unable to speak, he sang his story in his simple steps. Like the flamenco virtuoso, like the child in the fields of Bethlehem, Joseph's free movement flowed from within his own body with its unconventional gracefulness.

And when Joseph danced delightedly around our Christmas kitchen I used to think that the Lord of the Dance was tapping his foot too, and that, at least for those few moments, there was peace on earth.

Blessed Harrowing Hour

*Serious physical suffering causes not only despair but a crisis of
self-doubt – a questioning search for the true self before it is too late.
Yet amid the turmoil of the here and now there emerges a deep
consciousness of God.*

It is 2 a.m. I think I'm going to die. Because I cannot breathe. Who
will I ring? Have I the breath to speak? It is said to be the ultimate
panic – when breath and death compete? It was a long night. I will
never, ever forget it. It happened to me about three months prior to
writing this.

A brush with death, real or imaginary, can cut through our
pretensions and penetrate our defences. We begin to realise how
deep our darkness is, how lightly our demons sleep, how thinly our
virtues go. It is the time you look for a hand to hold, a time to reach
desperately for the raw comfort of faith. As I fought for breath, and
waited for the dawn, many recollections disturbed me fleetingly
but deeply.

How authentic is my life? How much pretence is there in my
presence to others and to God? Is my driving force for the Reign of
God or for the kingdom of Daniel? Have all my spoken and written
words come from my clerical ego rather than from my graced
human essence? Have I contributed more to the current troubles of
the Catholic institution than to making more accessible the lovely
light of God's abundant life?

There will be a blessed, harrowing hour in many people's lives when sudden shadows play havoc with the neat certainties that drive our decisions. And now, my hour had come. How sure am I of anything any more? How can I preach and teach with passion from an uncertain heart? Have I kept relentlessly busy so as to avoid facing the doubt and meaninglessness of my clerical life?

How do I get to know my true self before it's too late – that complicated, flawed self that is still a blurred face of our incarnate God? How do I let go of everything shallow that I cling to as a false validation of my life, to make God alone the wind beneath my wings? How long does it take to be truly authentic? Have I ever utterly and completely forgiven or loved anyone during the decades of my life?

On that night of panic, my dry, rasping cough matched my fierce inner distress. Something ultimate was pressing in. As it was with Jesus, I vaguely saw that without my demons, the angels could not come to comfort me. Could it be, I wondered, that this neglected desert of my soul was also my deepest, most real me, where God lives? Maybe this bleak and hurting place is where incarnation continues to happen.

That is why, for many of us, our inner shadowland is a fearsome place to go because for decades we have defined our goodness and truth by other criteria – our petty successes, our religious performances, our roles and titles, our public persona – all those utterly false indications of our real worth before God.

On the day that followed my dark night, I felt very vulnerable – both in the strangling in my chest and the struggling in my mind. My security, my sanity, suddenly seemed so fragile. I fretted about the complexities and contradictions of my life, its restlessness, its incompleteness, its hidden loneliness, its unrequited desire. And then, as I had to turn in to the core of my being, I wondered whether these shadows and tensions are normal enough. Maybe the very condition of our humanity has to contain within it a pathological frustration with our finitude, a daily dissatisfaction with our limitedness, a hunger for more.

Perhaps we can only ever glimpse a horizon that we can never really reach this side of eternity. It is a hard lesson to learn that this is the natural way of things; that we must find our joy within these frustrating parameters. Theologian Karl Rahner wrote: 'In the torment of the insufficiency of everything attainable we finally learn that here in this life all symphonies must remain unfinished.'

And yet, while true, this cannot be the last word. There is a deeper truth without which life would just be too hard to survive. It is the truth that there is a deeper power at work below our surface uncertainties.

The secret we keep forgetting, when the empty winds of despair blow across the winter wastes of our souls, is that it is always and only within those barren places that we can ever find the transforming comfort of a divine summer. Only then are we aware of God's astonishing bounty. We think we are impoverished in our small torments of insufficiency; but in fact, so often unknowingly, it is then we are on the brink of another breakthrough.

These sudden meltdown moments of unsolicited depth-reflections are usually forced upon us. They come from another place, unbidden. Yet they invite us into a deeper consciousness of God's paradoxical ways, where past brokenness, where our temptations to inner despair, are tenderly held and healed.

St Augustine described such experiences as 'bright darkness'. John of the Cross saw his dark night of the soul as 'a night of love'. Those moments urged the saints, and they urge us, to radical transformation. They are lessons about truth that prepare us for a happy death. Without such catharsis there can be no redemption, no new beginnings, no transformation in how we perceive things, in how we are present to each other on this fragile earth.

After a near-death experience, Abraham Maslow said: 'One very important aspect of the post-mortem life is that everything gets doubly precious, gets piercingly important. You get stabbed by things, by flowers and by babies and by beautiful things – just the very act of living, of walking and breathing and eating and having friends and chatting ... one gets the much-intensified sense of miracles.'[29]

Steroids, meditation and friends, twice a day, are now mending my recent distress – the physical and the spiritual – but not, I hope, before their green graces are sown in the soil of my soul. These summer blessings will carry, I know, new songs of what is possible, stars of courage for stalled hearts, and a tidal pull towards the golden shores of further adventures.

In 'Swan', the poet Mary Oliver wonders at that mysterious moment when reality shifts, when recognition transforms:

> *Did you too see it, drifting, all night on the black river? …*
> *Did you hear it, fluting and whistling*
> *a shrill dark music, like the rain pelting the trees, like a waterfall*
> *knifing down the black ledges?*
> *And did you see it, finally, just under the clouds –*
> *a white cross streaming across the sky, its feet*
> *like black leaves, its wings like the stretching light of the river?*
> *And did you feel it, in your heart, how it pertained to everything?*
> *And have you too finally figured out what beauty is for?*
> *And have you changed your life?*[30]

Be Bold and Choose

In the first month of the new year, millions are ready to overcome their natural fears of the unknown and throw off the habit of the familiar to embrace a journey that requires patience, determination and boldness to change not only the way of looking at life but life itself.

It is very early on the first day of the year. Intent and attentive, I'm sitting here at the window of my new home. The dark sea stretches before me. Out at the edges, the shifting shadows slowly reveal the shores of dawn. And deep at the centre of my being, I strongly sense the stirrings of a new beginning.

I both love and fear these beginnings of the soul. They require courage – courage to live differently, to disturb the routines, to reach beyond, to question our glib absolutes. We carry a great fear of change. But habit is often a false comfort. Everything about great religion calls us to explore depth. Everything about great souls does so, too.

'If you continue to do what you have always done,' wrote professional strategist Anthony Robbins, 'you will continue to get what you have always got.' When everyone is thinking the same, no one is thinking very much. The theologian Bernard Lonergan wrote of a human condition that blocks our openness to vision and wisdom. He reckons that we all have a personal 'scotoma', a blind spot that we develop to ward off knowledge that might upset our customary way of viewing things. Our relentless resistance to change results from the original sin of a personal and institutional fear.

Maybe the poet-priest John O'Donohue had something similar in mind when he believed that something inside us 'watches us play with the seduction of safety, and the grey promises that sameness whispers, and wonders if you would always live like this'. In the presence of life's mystery, it is wise to be uncertain. 'Sell your cleverness', counselled Rumi, 'and buy bewilderment.'

The new year is surely a threshold of transition. Fresh from celebrating the mystery of the Incarnation, our purified eyes are now open to astonishing possibilities – possibilities fired through pain. In spite of her awful torture and a life that was closing in on her, Sheila Cassidy could write:

> And so we must begin to live again,
> We of the damaged bodies and assaulted minds,
> Starting from scratch with the rubble of our lives
> And picking up the dust of dreams once dreamt.[31]

We need courage to shift our perception of things, to transform our consciousness of the mystery that we are. Where do we begin? One suggestion is to recognise that we have a choice about how we see things. One way leads to a more creative, abundant way of living; the other feeds all that is negative within us.

'Every time you make a choice', wrote C.S. Lewis, 'you are turning the central part of you … into something … different from what it was before … you are slowly turning this central thing … either into a creature that is in harmony with God, and with other creatures … or else into one that is in a state of war and hatred with God … and with itself.'[32]

Human thought and creativity have an astonishing power. It is God's imagination, the Christ-imagination, our imagination. They are all expressions of a divine presence. What amazing good news this is, especially at a time of widespread hopelessness. People are lost because they are disconnected from their souls' true spirit.

God created us, and became one of us for no other reason than to draw us towards transcendent shores of joy and peace and justice. These shores do not belong to heavenly landscapes. They are the shores on which we live – where terrorists strike, where recession hurts, where churches fail, where families collapse, where fear lives. In the face of the terrible evidence of a fallen humanity, beginnings are still epiphanies of God's faithfulness and of human hope. A beginning is its own truth. It is always a blessing and always timeless. Nor does it need an ending.

Beginnings remind us that we are all magnificent possibilities in disguise. We sense their muted insistence. One day, if we are ever to unfold into our God-given destiny, we must listen to this inborn whisper.

Life's best teachers warn us against staying on the circumference of our lives too long, or we will never know either ourselves or God. They remind us that we all have a mystical call to journey forth and undergo great testing in order to save our soul, and save the world. That, too, is the vision of Jesus. It must not get lost in ecclesiastical translation.

When we set out to begin again, spiritual forces that we cannot even imagine are unleashed both to support us and to frighten us. Because this enterprise isn't just a head-journey alone; nor is it the pursuit of perfect external behaviour. It is much more. It is what Christians call *metanoia* – a going beyond the mind, a reconnecting with the divine, a confrontation with our demons of doubt.

That is why Carl Jung taught that it requires patience, determination and boldness. It is a deliberate embracing of the darkness, of what he termed 'the night sea journey'. And this is an act of the purest courage. Theologian Martin Buber said: 'All spiritual journeys have a hidden destination of which the traveller is unaware.' Humble before mystery, R. S. Thomas agrees:

> I think that maybe
> I will be a little surer
> of being a little nearer.
> That's all. Eternity
> is in the understanding
> that that little is more than enough.[33]

Given our congenital facility for getting lost, Buber believed we need teachers to negotiate the journey of the soul. These guides will come in all kinds of disguises, at the most propitious moments. There is 'the teacher within' as St Augustine reminded us, there is the *anamchara* (soulmate) beside us, and there is the guardian angel above us. And all are the manifestations of the Gracious Mystery so utterly in love with us.

Too many die with their minds still shackled by a blinding, compulsive uniformity. Liberated thinking can transform the world. When you change the way you look at life, the life you are looking at will change too. 'Let a man in a garret but burn with enough intensity', de Saint Exupéry wrote, 'and he will set fire to the world.'[34]

In January millions are ready for a radical shift in their lives and in their thinking. The start of every year calls for a moment of stillness. This moment will reveal the possibilities waiting painfully to emerge from the soil of our soul.

The Senses Have It

It is often said that people are searching for meaning in their lives. But could it be rather that they are looking for evidence that they are really and truly alive?

A boy sat on the steps of a building with a battered hat by his feet. A cardboard sign read: 'I'm blind. Please help.' The hat held a few small coins. A man was walking by. He dropped a euro in the hat, picked up the sign, turned it around, wrote something on it, and put it back near the boy. Soon the hat began to fill up.

That afternoon, the man who had written the new words on the sign came back to see how things were. Recognising his footsteps, the boy said: 'You are the one who changed my sign this morning. What did you write?' The man said he only wrote the truth, but in a different way from the boy's words. The new sign now read: 'You are enjoying a beautiful day but I cannot see it.'

Both signs told the people that the boy was blind. The first was simply a statement of fact. The second reminded the people of the gift of their sight. One was about knowledge; the other about personal experience. One about the mind; the other about the senses.

Knowledge alone, ideas and concepts do not change us profoundly. Pure experience does. It is always focused, concentrated and non-dualistic. It attracts, persuades and convinces. After it, we see things differently. This may be a song, a touch, a film, a story, a note of love.

Our experience is pure when we hold no filtering lens, no preconceived notions. You cannot really experience reality with the judgemental mind because you are dividing the moment before you give yourself to it. You are not free to receive. You are in control of the outcome. Your fearful mind is in charge; you are not yet vulnerable enough.

The poets knew well that nothing can match the power of authentic experience. 'The secret of it all', wrote Walt Whitman, 'is to write in the gush, the throb, the flood, of the moment – to put things down without deliberation or framing – without worrying about their style, without waiting for a fit time or place … By writing at the instant, the very heartbeat of life is caught.'

Seamus Heaney, too, knew this. 'I rejoiced most when the poem seemed most direct, an upfront representation of the world it stood for … I loved Gerard Manley Hopkins for the intensity of his exclamations which were always equations of a rapture and an ache I didn't fully know I knew until I read him. I loved Robert Frost for his farmer's accuracy and his wily down-to-earthness.'

In their own way also, the mystics are great champions of human and spiritual experience. It is why they feel secretly sure about being chosen, invited and loved. In their efforts to explain their experience of God, they refer to an intense desire between themselves and their adoring God. There are echoes of the Song of Solomon in these lines from 'Draw Me After You' by St Clare of Assisi:

> Draw me after you,
> Let us run in the fragrance of your perfumes,
> O heavenly Spouse!
> I will run and not tire,
> until You bring me into the wine-cellar,
> until Your left hand is under my head
> and Your right hand will embrace me happily.
> You will kiss me with the happiest kiss of Your mouth.[35]

God became human experience: 'What we have heard, what we have seen with our eyes, what we have looked at and touched with our hands, concerning the word of life – this life was revealed … so that you also may have fellowship with us; and with the Father' (1 Jn 1:1–3).

When asked about the essence of his message, Jesus replied: 'Come and see.' Come for the day and experience the presence of my company. He gathered his life's passion into one moment of washing people's feet. He used the metaphors of bride and groom, weddings and intimacies, to explain the nature of union with God. All his words and works carried the experience of grace and the grace of experience. His own essential humanity was in evidence in that sensual experience of having his own feet washed by Mary's tears, dried by her hair and anointed with her fragrant ointment. In that sacramental moment of mutual presence, they both felt vulnerable, and they were both transformed.

Before he could believe in the Resurrection, Thomas relentlessly insisted on his need to touch the wounds of the Risen Christ. Deep healing and true faith are mostly found within the experience of woundedness. 'Until I put my finger …'

Authentic conversion is nearly always experienced corporeally and emotionally. Thomas' own wounds had now become sacred wounds. It was to make all our pain redemptive that divine love became wounded flesh. True to the Incarnation, Tertullian preached that the reality of salvation 'hinges on the feelings of the flesh'.

'The Holy Spirit can only be experienced,' writes Franciscan preacher Richard Rohr. God became flesh, the place of experience. Grace is always incarnate. Faith is that attitude that empowers us to experience in healing depth, all the hard and routine experiences that each day may bring.

All of this is not really surprising when we remember that God needed and desired to become our bodies, our senses, our emotions in time and space, so that divine being could be experienced everywhere, by everyone, not just notionally known by the few. It was with a view to experiencing an astonishing and redeeming intimacy with all of us that God created the world in the first place.

Mythologist and Catholic writer Joseph Campbell is of the opinion that people are not so much looking for the meaning of life as such, but for the experience of being more abundantly alive.

'Eternity has little to do with the hereafter,' he wrote. 'This is it. If you don't get it here you won't get it anywhere. The experience of eternity right here and right now is the function of life. Heaven is not the place to have the experience; here's the place to have the experience.'

The senses have it! We look at each other and see God's face, maybe faintly, every day. We taste something of the flavours of God's presence in everything that happens to us. There is a divine whisper in every sound; even the sound of temptation. No other religion dares speak of human experience like that.

Maybe our future resurrection will reveal that we have been experiencing it all our lives. We will have already felt it, 'proved on the pulse', as John Keats wrote just before he died. 'Heaven', wrote Fr Harry Williams in *True Resurrection*, 'will be recognised as a country we have already entered, and in whose light and warmth we have already lived.'[36] We will know well when we're home.

'Darkest, Meanest Mud and Muck of Things'

While Easter, with its beautiful liturgy, is a joyous feast, that same liturgy without sacrifice is false worship. The 'Triduum' is rooted in human suffering, and to encounter it is to encounter Christ.

Easter is painfully recognised and experienced mainly in broken places and broken people. It is with the flawed image, the damaged beauty, that God does great things. Only what is fallen can be raised. Here are three stories from friends about meeting the Risen Christ in deep disguise.

Gerry Straub is a famous American film-maker and author. In recent years he has visited Haiti many times, and often wept at what he has seen. 'On my desk in my library', he recently wrote, 'I have a mud pie I brought home from Haiti. I could never imagine being so hungry and so broke that I had to resort to eating something made from mud and contaminated water, something so vile it could make me very sick or even kill me ... Mud pies are baked in ovens of anguish and hopelessness.

'I will never forget my first visit to Cité Soleil ... The devastation, the tin shacks, the rotting trash, the spewing sewage, a little girl urinating in the garbage ... naked kids with bloated bellies running barefoot through pig-infested mud ... And then there was the fetid and nauseating stench from rotting garbage that was intensified by the blistering heat ...

'And then, all of a sudden and totally unexpectedly, something fun and joyful caught my eye and filled me with hope. It was a makeshift kite fashioned out of a plastic garbage bag. It seemed to laugh and dance in the Caribbean breeze … It showed me how imagination could lift the human spirit out of the muck of sadness and hopelessness … And so mud pies and kites came to symbolize the death and resurrection that is a daily event in Haiti.'[37]

Tom O'Connor, a Kiltegan Father, works in São Paulo. 'It was Holy Saturday night', he wrote, 'and the crowd was unusually small. It was raining as we tried to light the paschal fire. I had no torch so it was difficult to read the prayers in Portuguese. Nothing was going right. At the high point of the Church's liturgy, we were completely out of step with the incredible mystery we were so inadequately trying to celebrate. There was no converging of life and grace. Nothing was rhyming.

'With more faith than finesse I began the *Exultet*. Suddenly there were raised voices. Oh no! Not at this vital moment. My spirits sank. Up the aisle walked a stranger with two howling children hanging on to him. I felt distracted and quite irritated. Then the small congregation turned towards them. One of the children had taken ill. For the rest of the Mass there was constant and distracting movement at the back of the church.

'As I was quickly taking off the vestments to rush off to another church I noticed the stranger waiting for me. O God, just what I needed! More trouble and delay. Impatiently I turned to him. 'Father,' he said, 'I need to talk to you. Life has changed for me since my wife, the love of my life, recently died. I am now alone, trying to bring up these two boys without her. It is so hard.

'"Tonight we were sitting at home and the older lad said, 'Daddy, can we go to Holy God's house now?' It then dawned on me that it was Holy Saturday night. I used to be a catechist. I'm so sorry about the noise. But I do want to start again. The little sick one is getting better. They are both so happy that I brought them to Holy God's house."

'I was left speechless and ashamed in the presence of this man of faith. Tears welled up in my eyes. I will never forget that Holy Saturday night – the night I experienced in the depths of my being the very graces of the Easter liturgy I had just celebrated.'[38]

Gillian Coxhead grounds grace in her experiences as a mother of four sons, as a nurse in the accident and emergency department of a children's hospital, as a volunteer with her local L'Arche home, and in her association with a Carmelite community. She finds Easter love living at unexpected addresses in the streets of an ordinary town.

'It is [found]', she writes, 'in the moment of the group of teenage boys caring for their intoxicated friend – one holding the vomit bowl, another rubbing his back; in the moment of the elderly mother caring for her alcoholic daughter; in the moment of the elderly frail husband who wakes many times every night to turn his wife as she is unable to move for herself; it is the moment of the next-door neighbour who pops in several times a day to check on a sick acquaintance, and to stay a while even though there is nothing he can really do to help.'[39]

Three stories about the earthly reality of the heavenly life. Three raw and disturbing reflections that strip the covers from routine ceremonies, that reveal the human mess that must forever lie at the heart of real liturgy.

Theologian Karl Rahner insisted that until they are incarnated into the empty tombs of terrible nights – such as those in Haiti – into the bleeding wounds of humanity – like those touched by Thomas and Fr Tom in their doubts and even despair, into the compassionate Emmaus encounters with strangers along the risky roads of our lives, then all the paschal liturgies in the world are worthless. Liturgy without sacrifice is false worship.

The focus on the extreme pain of the Good Friday killing will forever keep before us that the Easter life is truly experienced in 'the darkest, meanest mud and muck of things' as the poet Emerson put it; that the Risen Life is something we painfully flesh into the routine and often shocking experiences of our precarious but ever-graced lives. This indeed is hard to take in. It threatens our comfort.

But there is no dualistic escaping the challenge of this weekend's *Triduum*. There are no half measures in our following of a totally and fiercely committed Saviour. We, too, are called to incarnate in our lives the liturgy of Easter, and, like he did before us, to actually become sacrificial resurrection for others.

The poet Harindranath Chattopadhyaya was once aware of the power of his work to move, inspire and 'win the hearts' of his followers. He rejoiced in this fine accomplishment. One day he realised this was not enough:

> *But now through new-got knowledge*
> *Which I had not had so long,*
> *I have ceased to be the poet*
> *And have learned to be the song.*[40]

Chariots of a More Sacred Fire

Every athlete in the London 2012 Olympics and Paralympics was going for gold, cheered on by the crowds. But there are also moments of self-sacrifice in competitions that most spectators don't see which stay etched in the memories of competitors.

1962. A wet Sunday afternoon in Cork. Six of us were lined up for the All-Ireland 100 yards sprint final. There was a puddle in my lane, just where I was trying to secure my starting blocks. This was a huge blow to my chances of a 'flying start', of 'going with the gun'. Even though recently ordained, I cursed my luck. Then quietly, the athlete in the adjacent lane (with whom I had previously trained) simply said 'I have no chance of winning this race. You have. I'll switch lanes with you.'

To this day, the memory of that generous gesture lifts my heart. If the roles had been reversed I would have been found wanting! Moments such as these give us hope in the human capacity for goodness and compassion. As it turned out, I only managed to take the bronze medal, but in retrospect I was enriched in a far deeper way.

Sport is about more than the medals, we like to think. Yet we see many examples of 'win-at-all-cost' attitudes, of drug abuse and cheating, of desperate and extreme measures taken to capture that euphoric moment of golden glory before the eyes of millions. Many athletes have freely admitted they would sacrifice years of their lifespan for the sake of an Olympic medal.

Yet every now and then, when our faith in the human condition begins to waver, there will be a different kind of golden moment when the human spirit triumphs over the fierce attraction for the limelight. In the teeth of competition, there will be a flash of grace, a light of compassion, when an exceptional athlete transcends the will to win, and freely chooses to challenge another more subtle competitor – the powerful, persuasive rival within, the ego with No. 1 on its shirt.

One such moment happened in the 1936 Berlin Olympic Games. Jesse Owens was watching his dream slipping away. He had fouled his first two attempts at the long jump. His blond German opponent Ludwig 'Lutz' Long explained to him how he could avoid a final foul by using a simple strategy. Owens took his advice and went on to win the gold medal with a final leap of 9.06 metres. And Hitler stormed out of the stadium.

Moved by the spontaneous graciousness of his closest opponent, Jesse Owens later said: 'It took a lot of courage for him to befriend me in front of Hitler … You can melt down all the medals and cups I have and they wouldn't be a plating on the twenty-four-carat friendship that I felt for Lutz Long at that moment.'

In his popular little book *Great Moments of Sportsmanship*, Paul Smith records this and many other moments of compassion, fair play and spiritual motivation that rarely hit the sporting headlines in a world so focused on the all-consuming but utterly volatile cult of winning. In his foreword to the compilation, Ryder Cup golf hero Paul McGinley writes: 'Intense competitiveness that also touches our soul is the essence of great sport.'[41]

It is to hidden moments and small miracles such as these that people often look for evidence of spontaneous goodness. They inspire glimpses of hope in a desperately competitive world, cameos of compassion in a ruthless society. These acts of altruistic love sustain the world. They are mostly unnoticed in the run of an ordinary day. Even when they happen in the crowded stadium, they have a shy invisibility about them. No chariots of fire await the heroes and heroines of the soul.

Why are some people capable of those astonishing gestures of pure compassion, these sudden epiphanies of love that never cross the minds of others? One afternoon in May 1988 on a hillside in Oakland, California, a grandson of Mahatma Gandhi was attempting to give us an answer. He pointed out that both as individuals and as a planet we are genetically coded for compassion, for *karuna*. 'Competition becomes combat', he called out, 'when compassion is absent.'

On the day he died, Thomas Merton spoke about the interdependence of all things. 'Compassion has no boundaries,' he said. Anthony de Mello points out that 'a spirituality named compassion' is in tune with the best tradition of Christian mysticism, Muslim Sufism, Hindu Advaita, Zen's atomism and Tao's emptiness. Compassion is pure when it makes no distinction between the subjects of its loving concern. It springs from an original intimacy that softens the edge of rivalry.

For Christians who believe in the full reality of the Incarnation, the Olympics can carry many other graced moments of meaning. The sheer perfected physicality of athletes, for instance, can reveal something of the power and beauty of God's own being. This belief in the humanity of God only enriches each one's viewing of the games. In the utter poise and beauty of an athlete's coordinated mind and body – the temple of the Holy Spirit – we catch a reflection of divine elegance, and the harmony of the Trinity.

A myth has it that racing angels entertained St Columba on Iona. God's delight was complete in the little skips and leaps of the boy Jesus over blocks of wood in his father's workplace. God is delighted too, St Irenaeus reminds us, wherever humanity excels itself. Christians see the Games as a celebration of both God and humanity – because ultimately these two mysteries are inseparable. Even heaven may tune in to watch!

Between them, the Olympics and especially the Paralympics offer sacramental moments of possibility and self-belief to inspire millions of oppressed, disadvantaged and hopeless young hearts. They will send signals for peace and liberation that reach out, through radio and television, to comfort and transform, if only for a moment, countless isolated souls in shattered communities where only war, greed and awful oppression prevail.

For all their inevitable flaws and failures, in this respect the Olympic Games have few rivals. They are watched by millions across our planet. The uniting power of the Olympic Torch tracing its way across our land, the imminent pageantry of the opening and closing ceremonies, the many symbols, rituals and anthems, the will to weave as well as the will to win – for all too brief a moment, this banquet of beauty blesses each host country.

Season of our Content

Autumn is the time of year to gather in the harvest and reflect on its bounty before hunkering down for the rigours of winter and the expectations of a new spring. When this time of consolidation coincides with a major personal anniversary, it becomes doubly a threshold moment.

To everything there is a season. Autumn yearns for connection and completion. It is a season of harvesting, of putting shape, order and blessing into things before the gathering up, the clearing away, the turning to a fallow time, waiting for the next awakening. It brings an open heart to what is yet to happen. Autumn is a threshold moment.

I experienced such a moment during the recent golden jubilee celebrations of my ordination. I suddenly saw it all as a sacramental threshold of my life, a gathering up of its bits and pieces, a celebration with those people who had shaped and enriched it, a pause to glimpse below the surface of decades of work and relationships.

All jubilees have elements of such profound realities, but the 'golden' one has a special depth, almost a finality to it. It is not quite like the final summation of the requiem eulogy, but it has similarities, a kind of concluding 'This is Your Life'. Reflecting afterwards on the celebrations, my friend Gerry said: 'In a way, last night's songs and stories were like a funeral – only the corpse was alive!'

I can only guess at what fills the hearts of couples at their golden wedding anniversary. Their past is vividly before them when the whole family gathers to celebrate. Their spouses, their children and their grandchildren are the very essence of their lives. The room is filled with faces of delight, with the vibrancy of wordless validation.

For me it had to be a little different. But many of the friends who had made me who I am, who loved and forgave me, who believed in me, were there like angels of my life – a living album of memories, an evening of unutterable gratitude. Sean, our musician that night, quoted Albert Schweitzer: 'One thing stirs within me when I look back on my life; it is the fact that so many people meant so much to me without knowing it. They entered into my life and became spiritual power within me … If we had before us those who have thus been a blessing to us, they would be amazed to learn what passed from their lives to ours.'

In a moving and profoundly honest reflection on the occasion of his own golden jubilee, moral theologian Dr Kevin Kelly quotes his friend Peter Harvey: 'I am either one with all Creation, linked indivisibly with everyone and everything else, or I am nothing but an illusion. It is not that I exist only in relationship; it is that I am relationship from the beginning. At no point can I step outside the web, for there is nowhere to stand.'

As I reflected that night on the remembered fragments of my life, and looked backwards at the criss-cross patterns of my choices, ministries and passions, what emerged was the vague shape of the fundamental option that I pursued, the main attraction and focus of my energies and efforts. I like to call it, as Michael Mayne did, the *cantus firmus*, the enduring melody of his magnificent life. It is when we find age, autumn or a golden jubilee upon us that we are drawn to reflect on the mostly unnoticed warp and weft of our decades.

Blessed John Henry Newman spoke about God's individual call to each of us to fulfil a certain purpose before we die. Infused into our hearts at birth, and purified, emphasised and celebrated at baptism, our role in life is to be true to that compelling commission to reveal something special about God. Without our commitment to that first and deepest vocation, there will forever be a thread of the divine tapestry missing.

There are certain threshold moments when we sense something of this destiny to which we are called. Such moments unsettle us. We long to hear the *cantus firmus* sound louder in our souls, for that vague horizon of our ultimate vocation to become clearer in our hearts. And there will always be one autumn in our lives when this restless compulsion for completion seems particularly compelling. Urgently we seek to see the whole picture while there's time, to accomplish the calling.

And so I'm just moving my home to another place. 'Another Place' is the name given by the sculptor Antony Gormley to his creation of one hundred cast-iron figures of men in the sea near Crosby, Merseyside. That is actually the neighbourhood I'm moving into. I will call my new home *Ait Eile* (pronounced 'ought ella'), the Irish words for 'another place'.

Why 'another place'? Gormley explains that his many creations, set in the most unexpected surroundings, are questions about the mystery of being, explorations into the meaning of our humanity, existential reflections around the essence of our lives. It is, he says, a call to the liminal spaces of our existence, an invitation to transcend our ways of being and seeing, bringing 'an extra dimension to our everyday common experience'.

Sometimes I see this present time in my life as the last chance to discover that other place where the light lives; that promised land towards which we are forever dedicated; that unfamiliar vantage point discerning the true north of our scrambled vision. And yet, is it really so unfamiliar after all? Maybe it is not another place that's new, but another way of being present in the place we have always known. Maybe the shores we search for do not belong to a foreign land, but were already glimpsed in the original vision of the divine child that lives in us all.

'Fear not,' said Thomas Merton to Karl Barth in a conversation about music and wisdom, 'though you have grown up to be a theologian, Christ remains a child in you ... there is in us a Mozart who will be our salvation.'

It is the child who holds and reveals the *cantus firmus* in us, who remembers God's dream for us. The task is to recover this child – through waiting, praying and above all through suffering. This enterprise costs us, as T.S. Eliot puts it, 'not less than everything'.

In a monastery in Braga, Tibet, the poet David Whyte was astonished at the compassion in the carved faces along the walls, lit by handheld lamps, carrying 'such love in solid wood'. He wished that all of us would allow the invisible carver's hand 'to bring the deep grain of love to the surface'. And is this when the inner child awakens too? Do we reach our original, essential vocation and destiny only when pain and joy become one within us? Whyte ends his poem 'The Faces at Braga':

> *Our faces would fall away*
> *until we, growing younger toward death*
> *every day, would gather all our flaws in celebration*
>
> *to merge with them perfectly,*
> *impossibly, wedded to our essence,*
> *full of silence from the carver's hands.*[32]

Threshold of the Soul

If we are to hear the silent music beneath the noisy traffic of our thinking, we need to learn how to leave the mind and focus on the senses. The distractions of modern life prevent us picking up the rhythm of grace.

At a Metro station in Washington DC a man started to play the violin. It was a cold January morning. He played six Bach pieces for about forty-five minutes. During that rush hour it was calculated that thousands of people went through the station.

After three minutes, a middle-aged man stopped for a few seconds and then hurried on. A minute later, the violinist received his first dollar tip – tossed in the box by a woman without slowing her stride. A few minutes later someone leaned against the wall to listen, but after looking at his watch began to walk quickly on his way.

The one who paid most attention was a three-year-old boy. His mother hurried him along but the child stopped in front of the violinist. Reluctantly the boy was dragged away, looking back all the time.

During the forty-five minutes that the musician played, only six people stopped and stayed for a while. He collected $32. When he finished playing and silence took over, no one applauded him or showed any sign of recognition.

The violinist was Joshua Bell, one of the world's finest musicians. He had played some of the most intricate pieces ever written, with a violin worth $3.5 million.

The event was organised by *The Washington Post* as part of a social experiment about perception, taste and the priorities of people. The inherent questions were: in a commonplace environment at an inappropriate hour, do we perceive beauty? Do we stop to appreciate it? Do we recognise talent in an unexpected context?

One of the possible conclusions to be drawn from this bit of research might be put in another question: if we do not have a moment to stop and listen to one of the best musicians in the world playing the best music ever written, how many other things are we missing in the course of our normal day? Do we forget that our senses are 'the threshold of our soul'? 'Listen, my child,' St Benedict wrote at the beginning of his Rule, 'with the ear of your heart.'

Another railway station; another musician; another busy mother and small son. This time in Leeds where a wintry wind was wailing down the empty platform. Linda suddenly realised that Iain had let go of her arm. In panic she retraced her steps. And there he was, hunkered down in rapt attention, listening to a scruffy, broken-down old man playing a lonely mouth organ in the cold rain.

Iain was offering the last 10p of his pocket money to his new hero, oblivious to the man's appearance. 'How lucky he is', he said to his Mum, his eyes shining, 'to be able to play such beautiful music.' Unlike people in Washington, Iain was listening with the ear of his heart.

Awareness is always about presence. But how often are we present to ourselves and to our environment in a distracted world where electronic multitasking rules, even while we're having a meal with a friend? From both within and without, that inner sacred place is continually invaded. Without this grace of space there will be no stillness for catching the cadences of the unfinished symphony beneath the surface of what happens.

One Celtic evening, the mythical Fionn Mac Chumhail and his warriors were having a discussion about the finest sound in the world. Fionn's son Oisín extolled the ring of spear on shield in the din of battle. Another chose the fearful cries of the stags and the baying of the hounds in the rising blood lust just before the kill. Yet another spoke of the song of his beloved as she played the harp to soothe her hero after a day of blood and gore. The wise warriors nodded their approval. 'And you, Fionn,' they then asked, 'what do you say is the finest sound in the world?' The mighty hero paused. 'The music of what happens,' he said.

We need to learn how to leave the mind and come to the senses so as to hear the silent music beneath the noisy traffic of our thinking, to catch the divine harmony in everything human. Close to our soul, we are called to become like human tuning forks catching the rhythm of grace.

The funeral memorial card of John Moriarty, the Kerry mystic, carried one of his reflections. 'Clear mornings bring the mountains to my doorstep. Calm nights give the rivers their say. Some evenings the wind puts its hand on my shoulders. I stop thinking. I leave what I'm doing and I go the soul's way.'

Along the soul's way we find the only places of encounter between our spirit and the Spirit of all life, between our emptiness and the universal flow of energy. It is along the soul's way that we hear and create the unique music that only we can hear and create. It is here that we come home to the God of harmony already within our hearts. 'God is always at home,' Meister Eckhart insisted, 'it is we who take a walk.'

If the present moment is the only place we can meet the incarnate God, will we be at home when God comes in disguise to find us? Are we always too distracted, seduced by other transitory attractions, to gaze at and recognise the Mother of all beauty – and to hear the music She is always making for us? There is something both funny and lovely about a verse in John Ashbery's 'At North Farm':

> Somewhere someone is traveling furiously toward you,
> At incredible speed, traveling day and night,
> Through blizzards and desert heat, across torrents,
>   through narrow passes.
> But will he know where to find you,

Recognize you when he sees you,
Give you the thing he has for you?[43]

It is as though a secret smile, a whispered assurance, a small melody lies hidden, like an impatient epiphany, in everything we encounter in the course of each day. Everything wants to draw us into the harmony of life. Everything is waiting to encourage and support us as we struggle, mostly out of tune, to get the timing right. Our monkey-minds miss the magic and the music of the moment.

There's a Joshua Bell playing somewhere always, in the most unlikely places. But we need to be aware. To stop running. To be here. *In Now I Become Myself*, May Sarton writes of the time it takes to be present to one's true harmony after years of distraction, of panic, of wearing 'other people's faces'.

O, in this single hour I live
All of myself and do not move.
I, the pursued, who madly ran,
Stand still, stand still, and stop the sun![44]

Grace and Radiance

Beauty is a pillar of faith, alongside goodness and truth. In an often dark world, we struggle to ensure that its importance and sacramental quality are not lost, for at the deepest level of our being we already know beauty and resonate sympathetically with it.

Across the ward, a man is struggling. His body is writhing on the chair near the bed. His right leg, arthritic and misshapen, is kicking against the cubicle curtain. Sweat edges down the furrows of his grim face. I want to help him but I myself am anxiously recuperating. Taut and strained with the intense effort, he makes one last concentrated twist. And before a passing nurse can assist him, he utters a hoarse growl of triumph. The battle is over. Calm now, he proudly begins the long and complicated manoeuvre of buttoning up his cardigan – the cardigan that Dan had just managed to put on.

Why do I still remember Dan's small victory when I have already forgotten the world records of the recent Olympic champions? It has to do, I think, with a certain simplicity, a concentration, a determination on Dan's part. It was neither contrived nor attention-seeking. It was utterly honest; it was total and it was real. It was, I now believe, beautiful.

Here, according to D. H. Lawrence, was 'a man in his wholeness, wholly attending'. There was no distraction in Dan's single eye as he battled with his uncooperative cardigan. If beauty is 'the product of honest attention to the particular' then I was privy to a small epiphany in a Tralee hospital that August morning. Did it, I wonder, somehow facilitate my own healing as I watched? And did an invisible healing grace dance through the ward at that moment? I do not know.

But what did dance through the hospital the following day, though not down our wing, was the newly-crowned Australian 'Rose of Tralee'. There was no denying the grace and beauty there. But not only there, shining as it was. The mystic in all of us will recognise the hidden shimmering at the core of everything, even the imperfect; the quiet music in all that happens, the world itself as sacramental. St Thomas Aquinas saw divine harmony, God's radiance and beauty in all of Creation.

That is why true beauty is always redemptive. In *The Idiot*, Fyodor Dostoevsky wrote that only 'beauty will save the world'.[45] Philosopher John Macmurray writes in *Freedom in the Modern World*: 'I am inclined to think that the worst feature of modern life is its failure to believe in beauty … If we want to make the world better, the main thing we have to do is make it more beautiful.'[46]

The Church has lost that blessed imagination. Beauty was always included with her two sisters, goodness and truth, in the traditional pillars of Christian faith. But the still virulent strains of Gnosticism and Manichaeism, with their fear of enfleshed beauty, have distorted the true vision and reality of Incarnation.

In *The Minister*, R. S. Thomas pulls no punches:

> Protestantism – the adroit castrator
> Of art; the bitter negation
> Of song and dance and the heart's innocent joy –
> You have botched our flesh and left us only the soul's
> Terrible impotence in a warm world.[47]

In his *Art and the Beauty of God: A Christian understanding*, Bishop Richard Harries, too, believes that all real beauty, no matter what its form, carries a divine radiance. He writes: 'the material and the immaterial, the visible and the invisible, the physical and the spiritual interpenetrate one another. The physical world becomes radiant with eternity ... This means that all everyday experiences have a sacramental character.' He also believes that this radiance of God 'can be fully present in failure and ignominy'.[48]

In *Waiting on God*, the French religious thinker Simone Weil wrote: 'Like a sacrament, the beauty of the world is Christ's tender smile for us coming through matter.' Drawn towards God, as we always somehow are from birth and baptism, we carry an unconscious attraction towards becoming small reflections of that beautiful smile. 'We do not merely want to see beauty,' wrote C. S. Lewis in *The Weight of Glory*, 'we want something else that can hardly be put into words – to unite with the beauty we see, to pass into it, to receive it into ourselves, to bathe in it, to become part of it.'

But why is this desire so faint within us? Because of a condition called spiritual blindness. In Alice Walker's novel *The Colour Purple,* Shug Avery reminds us how fed up God must feel when we walk through a field of poppies and fail to notice the colour purple. On the final Judgement Day, Rabbi Lionel Blue tells us, we shall be called to account for all the beautiful things we should have enjoyed, but didn't. Sin is blind to beauty. It lives in a flat world, it fears the edges, it does not notice colour. It is graceless. And it is graceless because it has no imagination.

'The imagination', wrote the Irish poet and priest John O'Donohue, 'creates a pathway of reverence for the visitations of beauty. To awaken the imagination is to retrieve, reclaim and re-enter experience in fresh new ways ... To put it in liturgical terms: each of us is the priest/priestess of our own life, and the altar of our imagination is the place where our hidden and beautiful life can become visible and open to transformation.'

Theologian and writer Ronald Rolheiser reminds us that at the deepest level of our being we already know beauty and resonate sympathetically with it. 'That Imago Dei,' he writes, 'that deep virginal spot within us, that place where hands infinitely more gentle than our own once caressed us before we were born, where our souls were kissed before birth, where all that is most precious in us still dwells, where the fire of love still burns – in that place we feel a vibration sympathétique in the face of beauty. It stirs the soul where it is most tender.'

My cousin, the poet Eugene O'Connell, writes about a beauty that took many decades to perfect. In 'Crossing the Fire', he wrote about my Auntie Nell and her husband, Johnnie:

> ... *So when Johnnie died we wanted*
> *Nell to sit on his side of the fire,*
> *Out of the way of the draught and*
> *The traffic up to their room.*
> *But she kept to the habit of*
> *their life together, and preferred*
> *The visitor to sit on his chair.*
> *Afraid that if she crossed the fire*
> *That there would be no one*
> *On the other side to return her gaze.*[49]

Lost and Found

The feelings of fear and abandonment that beset so many when they lose sight of the divine light within themselves are swept away by Easter's homecoming and are transformed.

Weary with work, with worry, and indeed with the world, Yvonne was weeping at the coffee table. 'All I want', she repeated, 'is to come home – to myself.' She had been dragged from her heart-centre by responsibility and anxiety; she was out of her true element. She longed to belong again – to herself.

After a terrible time of temptation and despair, of intense conflict on Holy Saturday, Jesus shone with his own eternal essence on Easter morning. Utterly abandoned a few hours before, he was now guided safely home to the fullness of his being.

Yvonne had temporarily lost her star – but her star had not lost her. Somewhere within her she never doubted that. She had always believed in some kind of invincible light within her darkness. This light was her innermost essence. It shone from Jesus at the Transfiguration. It shone again when he walked from the tomb. And it shines from us too when we leave the lost places of our lives to find the only love we feel at home in.

They start early in our lives – the feelings of being lost and found. And they stay all our life. I remember in the black nights of angry storms, the pale, smiling face of my mother behind the small candle. 'Shh, my love. It's alright. Mummy's here.' Then my fears would leave me. The dawn always arrived to find me safe at home.

When a frightened Jesus was distraught in the garden he, too, needed the human touch of his forgetful friends – someone to hold him and breathe brave love back into his faltering heart. He needed to hear his name whispered by those sleepy men, to be tenderly told who he was. As he stumbled around alone, already bleeding with fear, waiting for those who would soon kill him, maybe he was remembering those nights when he cried out, a small uncertain child, and his mother's calm face comforting his frightened soul, unknowingly preparing him for this dark moment. In *A Tree Full of Angels*, Macrina Wiederkehr OSB writes: 'That's you! You fragile, noble being. Little-Great-One. Yes, there are whispers of greatness in the frail envelope of your being.'

The perennial rituals of Holy Week – the washing of feet, the kissing of the Cross, the soul-stirring 'Exultet' – are not there to be celebrated as ends in themselves: the whole Passover experience is for the grounding and anchoring of us during the pain and passion of our lives, for our coming home to the wonder and challenge of our true identity in God. This is our hidden self revealed; the whole point of Creation, Incarnation and Church fulfilled in us. Before this transformation happens, many tears will fall along the way.

Richard Rohr OFM reminds us that St Francis embraced the leper on the road and tamed the wolf in Gubbio. But it is on the inside that our personal lepers and wolves must first be found and tamed. Until our divided self first makes friends with our own leprosy and wolves – the liar, the hypocrite, the coward within – there will be no peace around us. Our homecoming demands the greeting and forgiving of our demons too.

This process of our purification and transformation will take us up a mountain to a cross. This is a hard dying. And we need to be prepared for it. The only way to stay climbing that mountain of our own Good Friday is to allow God lovingly to support us with a passion. As it was for Jesus, it is the way of blind trust in unconditional love. St Elizabeth of the Trinity heard God's whisper, 'Just let me love and hold you! Let me take you home.'

The Rhineland mystic Mechtild of Magdeburg wrote:

God speaks …
When your Easter comes,
I shall be all around you.
I shall be through and through you,
And I shall steal your body
And give you to your Love.[50]

Possessed by this astonishing vision and love, we start to live without our former crippling fears. Physically, emotionally and spiritually we are experiencing the daily, radical grace of the freedom of the children of God. No longer trapped in the externals of our faith, we use them to enter into our true inner authority, our resonance, our transparency. Our hearts are now free. No wonder our faces shine when the Gloria bells ring, when the veils are removed, the lights flood the church and we sing with a visceral gusto.

There is another stride of soul to be taken in this journey home. It is this. In coming home to ourselves we come home to our world. There is really only one homecoming. 'We are already one', wrote Thomas Merton, 'but we imagine that we are not. And what we have to recover is our original unity. What we have to be is what we already are.'

'The earth itself is our home,' wrote theologian Karl Rahner. 'In his death the risen Christ has become the heart of this earthly world, the divine heart in the innermost heart of the world … we do not need to leave her, for the life of God dwells in her. When we want both the God of infinity and our beloved earth – when we want both for our eternally free home, there is but the one path.'

That is the meaning of the Easter homecoming – it is a coming home to the divinity in ourselves in an earth that is now established as our true home because it is the home of God. Our homeland is not in a faraway heaven any more: it is to be found at our own postcode.

The profound personal and cosmic celebration of the liturgical *triduum* is like a depth perception of the meaning of being at home. When we are emptied and purified, something glorious resonates within us.

The miracle hidden within the cosmic revelation of Easter becomes even more breathtaking. We ourselves are fashioned so as to give expression to that radiance. Within the framework of Incarnation, we, in our limitedness, complete the invisible beauty. We do it in the only way we can – by our daily integration of it and our often unaware expression of it. In our smile, our word, our touch, our bread and wine, something in us starts to shine.

This is what happened to Jesus when his human Easter-body fully radiated the divine light. He was blazing with beauty incarnate. They did not even know him.

Sign of Delight

A small, neglected church in a country town is easily ignored when so much else is going on around. But it tells a powerful story that is amplified in the season of Advent when the story of the humanising of God is revealed in all its profound beauty.

John Betjeman may well have been sitting on this same outdoor bench when he composed his quirky love poem, 'The Licorice Fields at Pontefract'. Two of us were sipping coffee and looking around us. Everything was totally ordinary under a bright autumn sky. A grandmother, sitting with her daughter, was bottle-feeding her grandchild. They were all smiling. Next to them, at another table, a man was smoking and reading *The Racing Post*.

An ambulance passed in the distance, its siren insistent. An ice-cream van, vivid in its colour and jingle, was surrounded by clamouring kids. The shops were busy. Two teenagers were laughing as they tried to hug each other while cycling past us. An argument suddenly broke out in a passing family. Just as quickly, it died away. A drunken man was sitting against a wall, his little dog staring at him intently and anxiously. Some folk were elderly, stepping carefully over the slippery autumn leaves. It was, as I have said, an ordinary street in an ordinary town full of ordinary people doing what ordinary people do – getting on with their lives as best they could.

Close by was a small church, locked, unattractive and unnoticed. We wondered why this was so. What had gone wrong? Why did it no longer attract people as it once did, or have anything to say, especially with the approach of Advent, by way of joy, encouragement for the town's inhabitants?

If we were asked by an interested passer-by for the story of that neglected church, we discussed two ways of responding. One way, the usual way, would be to describe it as the necessary refuge from a threatening world; therefore we must join it, become practising members of it, believe its teachings, obey its laws, overcome our sinfulness, so as to please a Christian God out there, and thus be saved.

Our questioner might point out that obviously such a message no longer touches people: that for some reason they do not seem to hear it, or need it now. Small wonder, she might add, it looks so lost and lonely.

The other way, we would then explain, the traditionally contemplative but forgotten way, would be to perceive that very ordinary church as the symbol of the holiness of the whole town, the sign that the families and individuals in every street are already a delight to God, exactly as they are.

Would this be too much for our questioner to understand, we asked – to see all the bustle in the streets around us, all the human commerce we had been observing, as the real presence of God, the shape and colour and smell of the God of Jesus, the human touch and feel and sound of the Christian God?

It is not primarily in the Church's teachings, we would continue, in the Scriptures, even in the Eucharist itself, that the blessed experience of God's presence is primarily accessed and felt – it is in the many happenings of the days and nights of our lives and of our world. This is a revelation too startling for many. Without the necessary grace of imagination, it is not possible to believe it.

We would talk to our new and interested friend about the God who is walking along the precinct here, disguised in the laughter and loneliness of the faces, hearts, minds of all those who, in their own way, try to live their lives as fully and as decently as possible; about a church that gently keeps purifying us of our deadly attraction towards what is destructive in our lives, of the fearful blindness that Christians call original sin.

The forgotten little church, we would explain, is really about a wonderful Christian belief that sees the world as the body of God, that sees our families and our communities as the home of the Holy Spirit. We would speak about the sacrament of conversation, the sacrament of listening, the sacrament of presence, the sacrament of the 'now' (although not in those terms).

We would explain that this little church was really there to remind Christians that they can, by their very presence, profoundly enrich the lives of others. There is no other non-violent way to bring peace to our hearts, to our town and to a world gone astray.

That is what this deserted church is for, if we but knew it. It is to celebrate every sign of human growing, flowering and authenticity, everything that unlocks our human creativity and imagination. It is a revelation of excitement. Given half a chance, it will touch us, and at very profound levels.

This mostly misunderstood good news fills our Advent days, when distracted people are again reminded of their wonderful story, of their divine potential. Unhappy in a society that has forgotten how beautiful it is meant to be, that has slipped its moorings and lost its direction, is there a way, we wondered, to restore such searching souls to the security of their unsuspected origin and destiny?

Fifty years ago, sitting on another bench, this time in the United States, monk and poet Thomas Merton, in a sudden moment of epiphany, looked around at the teeming streets of Louisville and asked much the same question: 'Who will tell these people they are walking around, shining like the sun?' That is the glorious role of the forbidding little church we saw in Pontefract that day – to be the utter guarantee of the shining presence of an incarnate God in all the community-making that goes on in the shops, pubs and streets around it, in the northern skies above it, in the good Yorkshire ground beneath it.

Maybe a postmodern world rejects religion, but this small church is on the side of the secular. It wants humanity to succeed, not fail. In an Advent reflection, James Hanvey SJ wrote: 'Humanity and

God are now inseparable and cannot be thought apart. We can no longer deny God without in some way denying ourselves. To exile God from the world is to alienate ourselves from our own truth.'

There is nothing new or fanciful about this truth. It is as old as incarnation. The whole heart of this driving vision of Jesus is expressed in the infancy narratives of Matthew and Luke, placed before us in song and story every day during Advent.

These Christmas stories, written well after the rest of the Gospels, are not about historical facts but create a subtle and beautiful theological poem that catches the essence of the humanising of God. 'In spite of so much terrible evidence to the contrary,' they are proclaiming, 'God has truly become human, and we are all now bright with divine beauty.'

What an astonishing revelation hidden in that unprepossessing place decorated with discarded cigarette packets, trampled liquorice wrappers, broken beer bottles – and straw.

Quench their Thirst

*The Eucharistic Congress took place in an Ireland still in shock from
the clerical child-abuse scandals. In an article written before that
meeting in June 2012, I believed the Congress had the
potential to be a catalyst for a process of spiritual renewal for
Church and people. Was I right?*

Two bishops and I were in an Irish cafe last year. We were talking
about the forthcoming fiftieth International Eucharistic Congress in
Dublin. I was suggesting a presentation and celebration of beauty
and power and new hope – something sublimely radical to lift
Ireland, even temporarily, from the unprecedented confusion into
which it has fallen.

There was no sparkle in the bishops' eyes. Only doubt. I spoke
about preparing one Mass to remember: the appeal of a Celtic
setting for it, the magic of Seán Ó Riada's sublime compositions,
the elegance of Irish dance and the depth of our traditions. Could
we not commission our best choreographers and dramatists, our
poets and designers, to combine in the crafting of even one
Eucharistic evening of utter native authenticity, one sublime
evening of memory and hope that would bring a small light to the
darkness of recent decades?

There was still no sparkle in the bishops' eyes. They were
thinking about what had happened to the Church in Ireland, about
the destruction of the Irish soul, about the death of something more

precious than the lost millions of euros of a dead Celtic Tiger. They spoke of the emotions of the innocent victims of clerical child abuse, of the anger of their families, of their own grief and helplessness.

Yet, here, I persisted, was an opportunity to fan a barely flickering flame, to touch what was deepest in the Irish psyche – a love of mystery and music, of myth and song, of heroes and heroines, and of a Mass that kept the dream alive, as it even had during the grim and empty Sundays of the penal laws. Before the eyes of the world, our faith would become an epiphany of divine and indestructible resilience, forged in the human smithy of feast and famine, of humiliation and courage, of despair and hope.

Now, nearly a year later, we await the unfolding of the imminent Eucharistic Congress in Dublin. Innumerable preparations nationwide are almost complete. Superb liturgies are promised. The Royal Dublin Society grounds and Croke Park will resound with worthy contributions from the best speakers in the land. The gathering will be ecumenical, youth-friendly and truly religious.

There will be theological symposia, catechetical workshops and opportunities for personal witness. And yet … will it capture our hearts? Will it take us deeply into the wonder of our own human mystery and the astonishing mystery of the cosmos? Will it fill Catholic Christians with a fierce desire to save the world because it is the body of God; to encounter injustice, poverty and violence, because attention to these sins is often sidelined in pursuit of liturgical purity and doctrinal orthodoxy?

Will the experience of the Congress move us all from outer religious routine to an inner and truly human recognition of a divine beauty already within every person, every community, country and continent – within every moment of true love and reconciliation between people of any race and way of life and religious belonging? Will it restore the universal gospel of compassion and equality clearly and definitively back to the heart of the Church where it surely belongs?

Beyond the pageantry and sacred music, the new translations and the old teachings, will the silenced song in Irish hearts, and in the persecuted souls of people everywhere, be given a new voice? In the midst of a predominantly clerical celebration, will someone be seen to simply kneel before the victims of heartbreak – children, women, sinners – betrayed by Church and society, and gently wash their feet?

'There is no consecration account, or passing of the bread or cup in John's gospel,' wrote Richard Rohr, OFM. 'Instead we come upon the story of Jesus on his knees washing his disciples' feet. It's really quite amazing that we never made foot-washing into a sacrament! John wanted to give a theology of the Eucharist that revealed the meaning behind the breaking of the bread, an active ritual of servanthood instead of the priestly cult that it has largely become.'

People across the world are in sore need of hope and healing. Life is incredibly extreme and violent. Fierce emotions wage silent wars in the hidden places of a suffering world. Despotic leaders and even 'developed' governments are destroying their own children in different ways. Will the Eucharistic Congress, spotlit on this world stage for a moment in a million, offer a counter-image of how life could be lived, one small but golden vignette of what a gospel community of mercy and acceptance looks like?

Will it be a gathering where sinners eat and drink before the saints do around the Lord's table, where women and men share equal power and authority in the inner circle of God's people, where institutional criteria will no longer blur the warm welcome of Jesus to all who have love in them? Christianity, not more 'churchianity', is what God's people yearn for now. Worship is worthless, theologian Karl Rahner reminded us, if it does not engage with these raw realities of our precious and precarious lives.

The moment that liturgy ceases to be a sacrament of life, of what is happening in our world – human, non-human and cosmic – it ceases to be Christian. That intrinsic connection with life was hopefully what Pope Emeritus Benedict meant when he said that we 'need a new beauty in the liturgy today if the world is ever to be humanised and transformed'.

Who will speak with passion in Dublin in a few weeks' time about Pope John Paul II's soul-stirring insights into the astonishing meaning of the Eucharist, intimately human and utterly universal? Whether it is celebrated in a family hut in Uganda, an infants' classroom in County Tipperary, or St Peter's in Rome, it is, he said, 'always celebrated on the altar of the world'.

'The Incarnation of God the Son', he wrote, 'signifies the taking up into unity with God of everything that is flesh and that is cosmic … the firstborn of Creation unites himself with the entire reality of humanity, within the whole of Creation.'

And all of this 'is consummated in the Eucharist', as Sally Read reminded us in her recent 'Homage to the body' reflection, 'as we absorb God with our very gut, flesh and blood'.

Beautiful Words

Nothing empowers us as much as words can. They may bring Christ's redeeming presence into our soul. But, like all manifestations of The Word, they conceal as well as reveal.

Words transform us. Beautiful words redeem our spirit. They find their way into places of hurt within us and heal them. They slip past the sentries of the mind. They are the kisses of the soul. They enter our bodies like Holy Communion. And then they do their fertile work. We live our days differently when we carry living words inside us.

These living words shape our lives in many ways, but mainly they transform our fear. *Through Corridors of Light* is a new collection of poems of consolation for times of anxiety and illness. John Andrew Denny, the editor, writes from the depths of his 'indescribable' nausea, isolation and despair. The onset of ME (Chronic Fatigue Syndrome) sapped his soul, energy, stamina and mental clarity. After Denny wrote to *The Tablet* about this planned anthology, some words on a card sent to him began the release from his prison of intense frustration. The simple, soothing, musical words of John Masefield's 'Sea-Fever' became a kind of escape from his trapped condition:

> *I must down to the seas again, to the lonely sea and the sky,*
> *And all I ask is a tall ship and a star to steer her by,*

And the wheel's kick and the wind's song and the white
*   sail's shaking,*
And a grey mist on the sea's face and a grey dawn breaking.[51]

Now he was able to go 'down to the seas again' and thus 'transcend the limitations that illness can impose on imagination'. And his new book was born.

Something within us is always desperate for the nourishment of words. In her lovely book *Saved by a Poem*, Kim Rosen quotes poet Mary Oliver: 'For poems are not words, after all, but fires for the cold, ropes let down to the lost, something as necessary as bread in the pockets of the hungry.'

So much healing happens when the soul is opened. We are healed by the words that let mystery in. Too many words, even religious ones, carry only hard and dry knowledge. They do not moisten or soften or reconcile. Poet David Whyte warns that 'This is not the age of information … forget the news.' In 'Loaves and Fishes' he writes:

This is the time
of loaves
and fishes.

People are hungry
and one good word is bread
for a thousand.[52]

Jesus used beautiful words to heal the fear that fills us when we lose direction, confidence and heart – words to warm us when we shiver on cold corridors with no familiar rooms to welcome us in. We need to hear them now. The whole world needs to hear them now.

But who will speak those words to us when the Church itself is in danger of losing its own soul? Where do we look for the vital voices of hope? We look within. Our hearts still carry the echo of God's music in Creation, of the Saviour's song in redemption. Too long have those hearts and voices been silent. To paraphrase the words of Hindu mystic Rumi, 'Speak a new language so that the Church can be a new Church, the world a new world.'

Writing recently in *The Times'* 'Credo' column about church worship, the Very Rev. John Shepherd referred to the need for 'incendiary words ... which are best able to offer perspectives we never imagined possible, never believed existed ... What is critical is the musicality of the words, their rhythmic development, their poetic symbolism, their ability to inflame our imaginations. That is why the words of our liturgies need finally to be in the hands of poets, artists and musicians'.

Hans Urs von Balthasar, theologian of beauty, believed that 'God needs prophets in order to make himself known, and all prophets are necessarily artistic. What a prophet has to say can never be said in prose.'

We forever search for more beautiful ways of expressing the inexpressible. At a service to mark the four-hundredth anniversary of the King James Bible, the Archbishop of Canterbury was reflecting on translations. Dr Williams spoke of the importance of choosing words that carry 'the almost unbearable weight of divine intelligence and love pressing down on those who first encountered it'.

When the old words failed him, Nobel Prize winner Rabindranath Tagore was 'at the last limit of my power' as he thought his 'voyage had come to its end'. Then, in his letting go into the unknown he wrote:

> *And when old words die out on the tongue,*
> *new melodies break forth from the heart;*
> *and where the old tracks are lost,*
> *new country is revealed with its wonders.*[53]

Theologian Walter Brueggemann calls for a poetic language where the Church's communication is concerned. When homiletic, liturgical and prophetic texts are all reduced to prose, 'there is a dread dullness that besets the human spirit. We become mindless conformists'.[54]

He writes passionately about our desperate need for 'a new word … a new verb, a new conversation … a new possibility'. There is a crucial time for the poetic word to appear. That time is now, he says, when, because of a 'fearful rationality' in our prescribed and routine rituals and proclamations, there is no room for the 'excitement of our hearts'.

In 'Finally Comes the Poet', Brueggemann quotes Walt Whitman:

> *After the seas are all cross'd,*
> *(as they seem already cross'd,)*
> *After the great captains and engineers have*
> *accomplish'd their work,*
> *After the noble inventors, after the scientists,*
> *the chemist, the geologist, ethnologist,*
> *Finally shall come the poet worthy of that name,*
> *The true son of God shall come singing his songs.*[55]

Percy Bysshe Shelley believed that poets rather than politicians were the unacknowledged legislators of the world while the much-loved poet-president of Czechoslovakia, Václav Havel, said that his success in peacefully overthrowing totalitarian rule was due to his choice of weapons – beautiful words. Our Church at home and abroad is in dire need of salvation. Here where I am based, in the north of England, from the land of the powerful prince-bishops, dare we hope for a poet-bishop to arrive soon?

Part Two

Show me a miracle and I will wonder for a moment.
Teach me how to see miracles everywhere
And I will change the world.

We are People of the Flesh

Rediscovering Incarnation; celebrating humanity

'God became human so that humans could become God.' Even though this beautiful truth was first expressed and believed during the early years of Christianity, most of us today have a different understanding of the Incarnation. At a huge cost to our quality of life, we have lost sight of this initial and exciting revelation. For some strange and shadowy reason the amazing mystery of the fleshing of the Word gradually became centred on a tougher, legalistic kind of transaction between God and a fallen race. Even today, redemption is generally regarded as a kind of rescue operation by God – a desperate last-ditch effort from outside to salvage a world gone adrift. The death of God's Son was part of the terrible bargain. When the core of Christianity is based on such narrow, sin-centred motivations, then the consequences are immense and, too often, quite destructive.

For instance there is a common belief that the Incarnation happened only because of human sinfulness – that is to say that original sin is the sole reason for God's decision to become human. I feel sure that this is profoundly misleading. God's people have suffered deeply because of this unbalanced but perennially popular theory. Another deadly legacy of a sin-based theology of redemption is the pervading dualism (see p. 139 for an explanation of this term) in Christian preaching, teaching and general understanding of creation and incarnation. By this I mean that over the centuries the whole point of the divine-human union has so often been misrepresented or even seriously missed. Instead of 'locating' God at the heart of God's creation, there is a persistence about maintaining the separation between the divine and the human, between grace and nature. Also, there are far-reaching implications for our understanding of church and sacraments and of our interpretation of many doctrines and teachings, when we rediscover some lost insights into the love and meaning at the heart of incarnation.

We are God's delight

We need to remember that Revelation is the amazing love story of God's desire to be intimately among us in human form. Full of intense compassion, God wished to create out of pure love, and then, in time, to become that creation. That becoming happened in Jesus Christ. In him it was revealed that God's heart beats in all our hearts, that all our bodies are temples of the Holy Spirit, that every creature is a divine work of art. How different that is to the awful picture painted for some of us of the angry God in search of vengeance!

Revelation is now seen to be about the beauty of being human since humanity is the 'raw material', so to speak, of God's presence in the world. Revelation is about the graced possibilities of humanity, graced at its centre from the very beginning. It is about God's desire to be known and loved in the humanity of Jesus Christ. It is about God's delight in being visible and tangible in human form. This is how it became possible for God to be close to us, to share completely in the experiences of creatures, the fruit of God's own womb. We can say with saints and theologians from the time of Christ, that the Incarnation happened not because creation went wrong at some early stage, but because in God's plan to share God's own divine joy with others, creation was first necessary so that Incarnation could take place. I hope that this does not sound complicated.

Think of a married couple. Out of their mutual love they conceive a child into whom they will pour their deepest care and affection. The child is 'full' of its parents, grown from the seed of their love, nourished in the womb of the mother, bearing its parents' image, reflecting so much of their personalities. The child is a kind of image of its parents. So too, in this renewed way of looking at the meaning of creation and incarnation, we are, in St Paul's words, 'copies of the glorious body of Christ', a kind of rough draft of the shape of God. In the *Office of Readings* there is a gentle exhortation in a sermon of St Leo the Great; 'O Christian heart, recognise the great worth of the wisdom that is yours, so that the creator may be shown forth in the creature and that, in the mirror of your heart as in the lines of a portrait, the image of God may be reflected.'[1]

When God was creating Adam, Tertullian reminds us, as do both Vatican Councils, it was the human form of the Son, the ever-present Word, that was motivating God. Adam was the long-term preparation for Jesus – a sort of prototype of the lovely redeeming Human One who was to come later. All of this we have tumbled to in the revelation that is Jesus. Now we know that all humanity is heading towards divinity. You and I are growing into God, as the mystics put it. In fact all of creation is already sacred, and reveals something of the glory and splendour of God. That is why we say that the event of incarnation has ended all dualism. Heaven and earth are forever mysteriously intertwined since the Word became flesh. And deep in our own inner being the kingdom of God forms an intrinsic part of our true nature.

The dearest freshness

The poets and artists are never tired of playing with this fascinating theme. Unlike many of the official teachers of religion, they have never lost the sense of wonder at the mystery of the indwelling of God in creation. For them, the smallest particle of creation becomes a window on God's beauty. Their intense energy is spent on revealing 'the dearest freshness deep down things'.[2] They see 'his blood upon the rose and in the stars the glory of his eyes'.[3] Kathleen Raine refers to 'the mountain behind the mountain' while Seamus Heaney reflects on 'the horizon within the horizon'. Like 'shining from shook foil',[4] God's splendour radiates from all creatures for those who stay blessed with the original vision of childhood. In the

19th century Matthew Arnold wrote: 'More and more, humanity will discover that we have to turn to poetry to interpret life for us, to console us, to sustain us … most of what now passes for religion will be replaced by poetry.'

The artist and the mystic use images and symbols to catch the firefly glimpses of the extraordinary presence of a 'Spirit of Wonder' beneath the seemingly superficial and ordinary. In his 'Letter to Artists' John Paul II states that 'every genuine art form in its own way is a path to the inmost reality of man and of the world.'[5] This reality is God. The world we live in needs such beauty in order not to rush into despair. Once we become sensitive to the meaning of the birth, life, death and resurrection of Jesus, then everything is changed. We see the world differently. We finally get the message. The human holds the key to God. 'Salvation,' as the Church Father Tertullian said, 'hinges on the flesh.' All things are made new. From now on, our vision and our focus will be trained on discovering the God of surprises hiding and playing at the heart of life.

Priest, palaeontologist and mystic Teilhard de Chardin, in *Le Milieu Divin* wrote: 'Through every cleft, the world we perceive floods us with riches – food for the body, nourishment for the eyes, the harmony of sounds and fullness of the heart, unknown phenomena and new truths – all these treasures, all these stimuli, all these calls coming to us from the four corners of the world, cross our consciousness at every moment. What is their role within us? They will merge into the most intimate life of our soul, and either develop it or poison it.'[6]

There is no dualism here. God is so intimately one with the world. We are not healed from the outside in. Grace is not something on top of, or part of, or added to nature. What we keep forgetting, or denying, or failing to understand is that *nature itself is intrinsically graced from the beginning*. Because of the revelation that happened at the Incarnation, we can now be certain that the kingdom of God is within, that the Holy Spirit is moving in our innermost being, that we look for God not 'out there' any more, but waiting to be discovered in our deepest self.

Even a partial awareness of this mystery of divine surrender to our hearts brings a challenging responsibility to the way we live.

Our style of life becomes profoundly affected by our belief that God somehow needs us to continually keep co-creating the world with him. We begin to realise that the kingdom of God is first built by us in each others' hearts. Our world view is immediately and radically altered. Our relationship to ourselves, to each other, to the world and to God is fundamentally impacted. In God we live and move and have our being. Empowered by the Spirit, nothing is impossible any more.

You are God's seed
A rediscovery of incarnation theology reminds us of the inseparable unity between God and us. It reminds us that all too often we fail to recognise this divine presence, especially in the least of our sisters and brothers. To miss this is to miss the whole point of Incarnation. Jesus is unambiguous about this when he refers to those who failed to recognise the divinity of the poor and needy, the loveless and the marginalised. St Symeon wrote, 'These hands of mine are the hands of God; this body of mine is the body of God because of the Incarnation.' The mystic Meister Eckhart preached, 'You are God's seed. As the pear seed grows into the pear tree and the hazel seed becomes the hazel tree, so does God's seed become God.' And St Teresa made the well-known affirmation, 'Christ has no body now but yours, no hands, no feet on earth but yours, yours are the eyes with which he looks with compassion on this world, yours are the feet with which he walks to do good, yours are the hands with which he blesses all the world.'[7]

Gone forever should be the destructive teaching that would see our time on earth as a brief testing-time of punishment in an alien place until our escape home to heaven. (Unfortunately this heresy is still alive in many of our dioceses and churches.) The Incarnation has revealed what true humanity is, and that it is to be realised not by running away from the world or turning our backs on it in indifference and fear, but by encountering, embracing and transforming it. Christ does not reveal what it is to be divine but what it is to be human. That our God-likeness might become complete is the purpose of creation. And the way to human fulfilment is to penetrate right to the heart of the world, in all its sufferings, ugliness and desolation as well as its joys, beauty and integrity. In Christ our humanity has undergone transformation. This transformation is not something added on to our nature – a divine layer on top of our humanity. It is rather the revelation of the intrinsic meaning of our lives. We are God's dream coming true. We are God's delight. God rejoices in our humanity and God is the energy behind every heartbeat of our lives.

Another way of putting this is to discern the activity of grace within our souls. At our very centre is the address of the Holy Spirit. God has taken up residence in our innermost place. We forget that the old distinction between the holy and the human has been overcome in the person of Christ. In Christ it is revealed that God's home is now in people. In him it is made clear that God speaks in and through the words and actions of all God's creatures. Our prayer and sacramental worship are the necessary means of remembering and celebrating this profound truth. We will explore in *Beautiful Sacraments* how Christian liturgy is the continuing revelation and confirmation of this deepest dimension of human life – namely that God's gift of self-communication and healing compassion is happening to us in every event and at every moment of our 'ordinary' lives.

One could say that nothing is outside the ambience of God's presence. Even before we begin to be present to others and to the world, we are already held in God's embrace. We do not, for instance, have a relationship with God *in addition* to other relationships. We experience God and relate to God, in and through all our relationships. Our relationship with God is inseparable from every relationship we experience. In *The Liturgy of the World: Karl Rahner's Theology of Worship*, Michael Skelley writes: 'We experience God most completely by experiencing ourselves and other people, and whenever we experience ourselves or other people, we also experience God. In fact, we give glory and praise to God most fundamentally by routinely living in a way that quietly affirms the original goodness to be found in every moment of life, no matter how ordinary. The renewal that is needed takes place when our daily lives become an implicit and unselfconscious affirmation of God.'[8]

Grace for all Seasons

We are here in the land of grace. Grace is always and everywhere available to us. It is only we ourselves who prevent it from transforming us more truly into that image of God in which we were first created. God's gracious gifts surround us on every side. It is important to remember that grace does not only travel on fine days. On wintry evenings, especially, grace is never far away. By this I mean that very often the greatest strides in holiness are made in the darker happenings of our lives.

In an article in *The Tablet*, 'Secular Life and the Sacraments: 1', Rahner puts the closeness of grace in this way: 'Grace is simply the last depth and radical meaning of all that the created person experiences, enacts and suffers in the process of developing and realising himself as a person. When someone experiences laughter or tears, bears responsibility, stands by the truth, breaks through the egoism in his life with other people; where someone hopes against hope, faces the shallowness and stupidity of the daily rush and bustle with humour and patience, refusing to become embittered; where someone learns to be silent and in this inner silence lets the evil in his heart die rather than spread outwards; in a word, where someone lives as he would like to live, combating his own egoism and the continual temptation to inner despair – there is the event of grace.'[9]

Grace has been offered to the world from the very beginning of its existence, by virtue of the fact that it is created as a potential recipient of divinity. Grace is, therefore, available always and everywhere, at least as an offer. The love of God does not become less a miracle by the fact that it is given to everyone. This extravagant offer is without conditions. St Benedict, in his advice to the cellarer of the monastery states that the person chosen by the abbot should regard 'all the utensils of the monastery … as though they were the sacred vessels of the altar'.[10] Monastic tradition tried to bridge the gap of dualism between the sacred and the human that plagued, and still plagues, the Christianity of our times.

For many of us, nature and grace are still seen as two distinct entities. The image of the world that this suggests is that of a two-storey house, where grace and nature are on separate levels, grace building on nature, but never really belonging to it or penetrating it. Today we are asked to make a 'paradigm shift', a total change in perspective, whereby the secular world is from the outset and always encompassed and permeated with the grace of God's self-communication. God invites us, and every part of the cosmos, to enter into communion with the divine Self, according to its own capacity. In his massive work *Theological Investigations*, Rahner wrote, 'The world is permeated by the grace of God ... The world is constantly and ceaselessly possessed by grace from its innermost roots ... Whether the world knows it or not, this is so.'[11]

Seeds of Glory

Celebrating our Humanity

From its very beginning nearly fourteen billion years ago, creation was already permeated and filled with God's compassionate presence. There never was a time or space in the history of evolution when God was absent from the world. In the person of Christ this tremendous love story has been finally revealed. The healing wholeness has been accomplished. The human is now the home of the divine. What was begun in creation is completed in the Incarnation. The long-awaited moment has brought a stunning vision to human awareness. The search for God is no longer a dualistic journey outwards; it is the recognition of what is already throbbing within us. That is what we celebrate in the sacraments. But the immediacy of the eternal God keeps slipping our mind. It is divine power that energises our daily lives. Grace is life fully lived.

Moral theologian Fr Sean Fagan explains in 'Sacraments and the Spiritual Life', an article in *Doctrine and Life*, that Francis of Assisi, with his eyes of faith, had no difficulty with this kind of vision. For him the sun and the moon, fire and water, animals and humans, all spoke of God. As Christians, this insight is offered to all of us. The smallest particle of creation is a theophany, a revelation of God – the acorn, the grain of sand, the shrill siren of a passing train. All too often our act of seeing stops at appearances, failing to explore the love and meaning at the core. We need eyes to read the wind, the stars, people's faces as they pass by, in such a way as to go below the surface. But there are moments which stand out from all others, moments which come like a gift, moments when 'the focus shifts and a single leaf becomes a universe, a rock speaks prophecies and a smile transforms a relationship.'[12]

We call such moments sacred, because in them we glimpse something of the sacredness of life, the wonder of God. Following on from this, Fr Fagan writes: 'What needs to be emphasised is that our sacramental celebration becomes more meaningful when it is seen as a high point, a peak moment, a special occasion in a life that is already sacramental in its own right. The sacraments are of a piece with the rest of life and reality, not eruptions from a different world. In this sense it is more helpful to approach them from the context of life as a whole. They are moments of insight, bringing home to us, each in its own way, the deeper meaning of our life and destiny. The sacraments declare forth what is otherwise hidden in the darkness of the world, in the routine of everyday. They bring into focus and draw our attention to what we tend to ignore and lose sight of when we are busy about many things.'[13]

In time and space, in ordinary signs and symbols, the scattered fragments of our lives are gathered up and for a moment given meaning in the light of Christ. John Macquarrie writes, 'In the word and sacraments, the divine presence is focused so as to communicate itself to us with a directness and intensity like that of the Incarnation itself.'[14]

Encompassed by love

People are sometimes a little anxious at this kind of teaching. Forgetting what happened in the Incarnation, they fear that such theology is 'too human'. They have the uneasy feeling that God is somehow diminished when creation is raised to such a holy state. Are parents jealous when their children are honoured? We are so unfamiliar with unconditional love. Most of us have experienced only conditional acceptance. We are gently challenged by the Incarnation to trust in the extravagance of the divine heart. At all times this beautiful world is encompassed by God's love.

Even if we wished we would be hard put to avoid the experience of God. The experience of God is practically inescapable. We cannot help coming into the embrace of divine compassion whenever we experience anything. Skelley writes: 'We do not sometimes have experiences of love, fear, ourselves, or anything else and then also have experiences of God. The basic, original experience of God, on the contrary, is the ultimate depth and radical essence of every personal experience.'[15] Until this is clearly understood it is very difficult to truly grasp the essential meaning of worship or liturgy or the celebration of the sacraments. Before the Sunday Eucharist can be a celebration of spiritual and joyful healing and empowerment for us, every human encounter must be seen as somehow an encounter with God.

The Irish poet Patrick Kavanagh finds God in the scattered fragments of each day. Probing into the commonplace he contemplated the eternal. Writing about the loving mystery that is easily ignored or overlooked because of its hidden nature, Karl Rahner feels the need to 'dig it out, so to speak, from under the refuse of the ordinary business of life'. This detection of the quiet gift of the abundant life, waiting to be discovered in the shadow and light of each night and day, is the work of the mystic. There is no doubt that we are called to awaken and nourish the mystic already alive and well within each one of us. To deny this child of wonder within us, to refuse to acknowledge our lonely mystic, is to reduce our life to a grey dullness, to starve our imagination, to stifle the Holy Spirit.

Mysticism has to do with the search for the hidden love and meaning, for the experience of the abiding, absolute mystery of God, in the ordinary things that happen during our days and nights. This is particularly true of the positive and wonder-filled moments that come our way. What needs to be emphasised is that, on our part, a certain attuning and sensitising is necessary. We must work at this kind of vigilant awareness. De Chardin spoke of acquiring the 'skills' of perfecting the sacramental imagination. Beyond looking, even seeing, there is the graced gift of 'recognising'.

The beauty, joyfulness, or goodness of a particular experience might well be a compelling revelation of the presence of God. For example, experiences in which we witness something majestic, celebrate with a faithful friend, are overcome by the immensity of the ocean, are unconditionally loved by a parent, wonder at the splendour of the stars, play with a child, marvel at the grandeur of a mountain range, or delight in the passion of a lover, can all be powerful experiences as we recognise the absolute mystery. Most powerful of all, perhaps, is when we can discern the hand of God in the painful, restless and empty seasons of our decades on this earth. Our desire to be increasingly attentive to the presence of God would lead us to contemplate moments such as these and all the everyday instances of hope, joy, peace, beauty, and goodness that we so often take for granted.

If we cannot see God in the ordinary events of life, Rahner holds, then we cannot expect that we will suddenly be able to see God when we gather for worship. To the extent that we have a heightened awareness of the absolute mystery in all the joys and sufferings of life, we will have little trouble in finding God in the liturgical assembly. Before worship can be an explicit experience of God, daily life must be an explicit experience of God. This theologian is convinced that we all carry a child-mystic within us; that mysticism, in its real meaning, is not as remote as we often assume; that Christians must become mystics who are attuned to the mysterious light that shines behind and through all that happens.

Original beauty

There can only be a realistic passion for the possible when we are convinced of the divine power that drives our energies beyond limited horizons. Until we re-vision our theology, substituting a more enlightened model of revelation for the dualistic thinking that has dominated our teaching and preaching for centuries, we will never succeed in making that liberating 'paradigm shift' that transforms us to the core of our lives. And until our theology is renewed to bring it into line with the truest traditions of the church we will never understand the divinity of humanity. We will forever hesitate about transcendence and immanence, following endlessly uncertain cul-de-sacs about false distinctions between 'God and man', and falling into ambiguous traps about nature and grace.

These 'theological glimpses' are but a faint reflection of the thinking of the finest Christian theologians of all time. This general interpretation of incarnational theology is drawn, in particular, from the work of Karl Rahner, widely regarded within the church as the most influential thinker of these centuries, and from the work of St Thomas Aquinas, Doctor of the Church and still the Roman Catholic theologian of divine revelation. I end this section with a number of revelatory quotations from the latter: 'Every creature participates in some way in the likeness of the divine essence ... In all creatures there is a footprint of the Trinity.' 'God is not threatened when creation is honoured.' 'To hold creatures cheap is to slight divine power ... In a certain sense, one can say that God is more closely united to each thing than the thing is to itself.'

Throughout *Sheer Joy: Conversations with Thomas Aquinas* theologian Matthew Fox uncovers many lovely insights of the 'Angelic Doctor'. Referring to the energy and image of God in everything, Aquinas writes, 'All natural things were produced by the divine art, and so may be called God's works of art ... Just as flaming up comes with fire, so the existence of any creature comes with the divine presence.' God's delight in the interconnectedness of creation is also made clear. 'God contains all things and hugs them in an embrace insofar as all things are under the divine providence ... The Godhead is both a place and foundation and chain connecting all things.'[16]

Aquinas had such a profound sense of the holiness of life, a sense that has largely been destroyed because of a dualistic mentality that dominated later theology. 'It is not possible to find something that does not have (some) being and perfection and health ... There is nothing that does not share in goodness and beauty.' Regarding beauty and light he had much to say. 'God is beauty itself, beautifying all things ... with a holy beauty ... God puts into creatures, along with a kind of sheen, a reflection of God's own luminous ray, which is the fountain of all light ... From this Beautiful One, beauty comes to be in all beings, for brightness comes from a consideration of beauty.'[17]

There is something earthly and deeply satisfying in the incarnational approach of Aquinas. He stirs memories in us of the intoxication of the Celtic people in their awareness of God's delight. There is a sense of divine ecstasy in his description of creation. 'The Godhead, who is the cause of all things, through its beautiful and good love by which it loves all things, according to the abundance of divine goodness by which it loves all things, becomes outside of itself.' Divine love produces ecstasy. Aquinas inspires us with the poetry of his expression. Referring to those who are restored in God's spiritual 'sweetness', he writes, 'But what is more, they will be drunk, meaning their desires will be filled beyond all measure of merit. For intoxication is a kind of excess, as the *Song of Songs* says, "my beloved, you are drunk with love".'[18] May the artist and mystic in all of us reach that moment one day. The composer Schuman, for instance, was drunk with the music within him. During the last year of his life he wrote over 140 songs, more than his total tally until then. 'I will die,' he said to his wife Clara, 'like the nightingale, from singing.'

Beautiful Sacraments

They celebrate the divine presence already in our hearts

It is common, unfortunately, for preachers to talk about the sacraments in terms of offering grace to graceless people. This presumes, to a greater or lesser extent, that those who do not belong to the sacramental life of the church are without grace. There is a hollow ring to that supposition. It carries no echo, except that of sadness or self-doubt, within people's spirit. In such a proclamation there is no good news. And this, in turn, contributes to the phenomenon of the faithful departing from our communities. These are the people who have given up on formal religion but who long for an authentic spirituality. They have given up because they see no relevance between their lives and their religious practices, between nature and grace. Instead of finding inspiration, strength and empowerment, they experience confusion and irrelevance.

Grace does not designate a 'supernatural' area standing above and beyond created nature: it refers, instead, to that significant ground of all being which circumscribes and supports the horizon and depth of everyday experience. The liturgy is rich with expressions of this truth. The Eucharistic Prayers and the Prefaces, the form of our sacramental celebrations, the prayers of the Roman Ritual, all point to the universal presence of God in and around everything, as the fountain, source and sustainer of creation, 'of all life and holiness'.[19] Indeed how remarkably striking are the words that ring out with joy and confidence in the preface of Christmas III:

> *Today a new light has dawned upon the world;*
> *God has become one with humanity*
> *and humanity has become one again with God.*
> *The eternal Word has taken upon himself our earthly condition*
> *giving our human nature divine value.*
> *So enchanting is this communion between God and humanity*
> *that in Christ the world bestows on itself*
> *the gift of God's own life.*[20]

Grace is the innate capacity each one possesses to relate, forgive, encounter suffering, create, invent, imagine, endure, explore – indeed to do anything which is a positive option for love and growth. Grace is the context and potential transformation bound up in every moment of being and becoming, in every desire and achievement of authentic self-realisation. While we are obliged to believe in the absolute giftedness of grace, we can affirm too, with equal force, in the words of the brilliant theologian, Piet Fransen, that 'grace sets our deepest humanity free, precisely because it restores our most authentic humanity to us and by this means, humanises us to an eminent degree ... Properly speaking, we do not receive grace; we do not possess it as something foreign to us, or as something entering into us from the outside; for we *are* our grace. As Caesar wisely observes in Thornton Wilder's *Ides of March*: "I seem to have known all my life, but have refused to acknowledge, that all, all love is one, and that the very mind with which I ask these questions is awakened, sustained and instructed only by love"[21].'[22]

Sacraments of what happens
Whether we use the word 'sacrament' in terms of Jesus Christ, of the Church or of the individual rites that vary between traditions, we are talking about celebrations of ordinary and extraordinary life, about validating the authenticity of human experience and about

the individual and communal need for purification, discernment and transformation in the vicissitudes of our fragile existence. The first step towards a deeper understanding of sacraments is to see them in the context of a world already permeated and filled with God's presence.

The art is to enable people to become what they already are. The phrase 'Receive who you are' accompanied the offering of the holy bread at the Communion of the Mass in the early years of Christianity. You are the Body of Christ. Grace is orientated to our humanity in its fullness. God's basic gift to people is the lives they live and the good earth from which they make their living. In *The Furrow*, James Mackey writes: 'The life which is now being called God's primordial and perennial grace to man is precisely the life of everyman's everyday experience. It is man's working and eating, walking in the fields or on the seashore, playing for his team or dancing in his club, sleeping with his wife or talking with his friends, suffering the slings and arrows of outrageous fortune or holding out a helping hand to his fellow man, deciding what is best with the best guidance he can get and getting up for Mass on Sundays. All that is grace.'[23]

Instead of superficially perceiving those 'outside the church' as somehow unfinished or incomplete, or even nameless or neutral, or worse still, as blind and lost, perhaps, following the sensitivity of Jesus to all that his Father has created, our church will, one day, find its very meaning and mission in proclaiming the essential holiness of all people, the sacred heart of all creation. Is God diminished when God's family is sanctified? Does the church lose when the world grows more truly healthy? Is not the very work of the Spirit to reveal the innate worthiness and beauty of matter? Is it not only in the arena of the life of the world that sin and evil can be encountered and transcended?

In 'Paradigms of Sacramentality' Christopher Kiesling examines the notions of grace and nature. 'Christian faith is born of the experience of Jesus Christ, a man who was born, lived, suffered and died like other people, yet in whom God was reconciling all things to himself. Through Jesus Christ, people were given the insight that in ordinary human existence, its joys and sorrows, its hopes and disappointments, its daily activities like eating and relaxing, conversing and enjoying companionship, its use of things and interaction with people, God is at work transforming people into his children in whom he wishes to dwell in a communion of life.'[24]

The Vatican Council's document *The Church in the Modern World* makes it clear that in the past we overemphasised the notion of two distinct worlds, one sacred and one profane. Gregory Baum, a *peritus* at the Council, expresses, in *Man Becoming*, his special insight in this way: 'The radical distinction between the sacred and the profane has been overcome in the person of Christ. In Christ it is revealed that the locus of the divine is the human. In him it is made manifest that God speaks in and through the words and gestures of people. The Christian way of worship, therefore, can no longer consist in sacred rites by which people are severed from the ordinary circumstances of their lives. Christian liturgy is, rather, the celebration of the deepest dimension of human life, which is God's self-communication to people. Liturgy unites people more closely to their daily lives. Worship remembers and celebrates the marvellous things God works in the lives of people, purifies and intensifies these gifts, makes people more sensitive to the Word and Spirit present in their secular lives. The sacraments of Christ enable people to celebrate the deepest dimension of their lives, namely, God's gift of God's self, in a way that renders the dimension more powerful.'[25]

I never cease to be amazed at such glimpses into the meaning of revelation. And whenever we share it with others, the reaction is similar. After talks, workshops and presentations about such an understanding of the mystery of incarnation, invariably there will be those who say something like, 'What you have said is not new. We have always known it in our hearts. We have never doubted the sacredness of our lives, of our childbearing and our daily work, of our struggles to survive and grow, of our efforts to forgive and start again. Our hearts have always told us that these are holy tasks. All that's new is that now we have heard it said.' What a deep transformation it would trigger off around the Christian world were this good news to be proclaimed wherever the people are gathered around the table of the Lord.

The curse of dualism – it is anti-incarnation
At this point a brief reference to the phenomenon we call 'dualism' may help the reader. Dictionaries offer many definitions, and many of them refer to a spiritual type of dualism. In this instance, its presence is regarded as destructive because it strikes at the unity of the divine and human that was revealed at the first Christmas. There are various stages in the evolution of God's self-revelation in creation and incarnation, where the original design of divine enfleshment can get lost, where wrong turnings can be taken, where the first sublime purpose can be gradually sidelined, where a deadly dualism of separation can set in. Dualism is a terrible cancer in the various bodies of divine revelation: it is the pernicious virus that destroys the clarity of God's desire and decision to become human. And it continues to be a festering wound in the body of the churches today – because it does not recognise the unity and intimacy between heaven and earth that lies at the heart of Christianity.

Because dualism is so full of sin and so antipathetic to the true heart of God's revelation in Christ, and of Christ's embodiment in the Christian Church, it needs careful watching. According to theologian Edward Schillebeeckx, dualism denies the intrinsic value of the created order, a value enshrined in a once-powerful Jewish–Christian tradition of the blessedness of all creation. It denies that God willed the world as it is, or willed human beings as they are. To be finite, such views would hold, or to be vulnerable, to fail, to die, arises from a basic human flaw or from some primal sin. Therefore, dualism would insist, the true form of our humanity is set in a previous lost paradise or in a future age after this world has ended. Dualism would hold that to be human is to go radically astray, to be wrong-footed from the start, to be flawed in our finitude, from a first sin at the beginning of time. It refuses to accept ignorance, mortality and mistakes as the normal condition of humanity.

This dualism, to my mind, is the main reason for the disturbing difficulties that face the Catholic Church today. Bede Griffiths, for example, saw the essence of all religious progress as one from 'dualism' to 'non-dualism'. Another fine European theologian,

Dorothee Sölle, defines dualism as that which sees human power and creativity as somehow detracting from God's power in our world, as though mature parents would be jealous of their children's self-esteem and self-confidence. Human creativity can never detract from the power of the divine presence, since its source is one and the same.

Sölle senses the need to develop a spirituality of creation. Old religious language, outdated literalism and conventional images of God and humanity must develop, for instance, from 'otherness' to 'sameness'; from 'infinite distance' to 'mystical union'; from 'God as wholly other' to 'God within us'; from 'obedience to God' to 'empowerment by God'; from 'Father, Judge' image to 'depth, source, creative-being'. Sölle writes of three essential dimensions of a spirituality of creation – the sense of wonder, the human capacity to perceive beauty, and the presence of joy.[26]

Sacraments celebrate our lives

And so we understand the individual sacraments as privileged moments of ultimate meaning, as windows of deep disclosure, as holy X-rays that reveal the true condition of a person's or a community's inner, spiritual health. Leaving aside an often misleading or even damaging and dualistic catechesis about the sacraments, what they basically do is to take the earthly realities of our human existence – birth, reconciliation, sickness, love, the need to worship, commitment, death – and to the eyes of faith they show forth the deeper meaning hidden within, the silent activity of the Spirit, gradually sanctifying and redeeming every aspect of daily life until the time when God will be 'all in all'. In his famous *Christ the Sacrament*, Schillebeeckx reminds us that whatever is lived out in an everyday manner outside the sacraments, grows to its full maturity within them. The anonymity of everyday living is removed by the telling power of Christ's symbolic action in and through his Church. Therefore, the sacraments cannot be isolated from the organic unity of whole, human, persevering Christian life.

To take one example: Referring to someone who comes to celebrate the Eucharist, Karl Rahner writes in 'Secular Life and the

Sacraments: 2': 'He offers up the world under the form of bread and wine, knowing that the world is already constantly offering itself up to the incomprehensible God under its own forms, in the ecstasy of its joy and the bitterness of its sorrow. He looks, praising, at God's ineffable light, knowing that this vision takes place most radically where eyes weep tears of blood, or glass over as they see the approach of death. He knows that he is proclaiming the death of the Lord, in as much as this death, once died, lives on always in the world, is built into the innermost centre of the world, and is truly enacted again in that man, who, whether he knows this expressly or not, "dies in the Lord". He knows that he is proclaiming at Mass the coming of the Lord, because the Lord is already realising his coming in the world in everything that drives the world on towards its goal. He receives under holy signs the true Body of the Lord, knowing this to be worthless were he not to communicate with that Body of God which is the world itself and its fate; he partakes of the one Body so as to remain always in communion with that other Body in the reality of his life.'[27]

To be sacramentally literate, according to spiritual writer Fr Hugh Lavery, we would move beyond the constraints of time, space, numbers and immediacy. While always relying on the tangible elements of the earth for their matter and form, the essence of sacrament, whether as applied to the Saviour, to the Church, or to baptism or Eucharist, is to point away from itself, as Jesus did, to move out into a wider field of reality, to embrace within its symbolism that which could otherwise never be brought home.

Where reconciliation is concerned, for instance, there is the vital need to remember that we are all, always, forgiven for everything by virtue of the one and only sacrifice of Jesus Christ in his Passover. If anything is 'left over' to complete the mystery, as St Paul implies, it is that we forgive each other, always and everywhere, as we solemnly pray in the 'Our Father' before receiving Holy Communion at Mass. The sacrament of reconciliation is not about begging for 'another' divine forgiveness, a 'second' type of atonement between Church and penitent, between God and sinner. Nor is it a holier, more divine reconciliation, above and beyond human forgiveness. Not everyone is aware of this, namely the true significance and necessity of the communal celebration of this sacrament.

What is celebrated is the forgiving presence of the indwelling Blessed Trinity in each human being. This is first expressed and shared in whatever ways are appropriate to the people concerned. It may be within a community, a family, a friendship or within one human heart. What is important to believe is that wherever and whenever it happens, there, and only there, is the event of grace, the power of the Spirit, the infinite and complete energy of God. Nothing else is needed. At that moment the Godhead is fully fleshed, the incarnation continues, the once-for-all paschal mystery is made present, the Holy Spirit is audible and tangible. There is no need for a two-tier hierarchy of forgiveness – one human, one divine. And yet, throughout Christian countries, Churches, parishes and schools, our liturgical preaching and sacramental catechesis often convey a confusing double-decker kind of approach to grace and nature, to the human and the divine.

Again, the sacraments do not confer a grace that was absent. Sacraments proclaim and enable us to own a love that is already present to us. A sacrament celebrates the Lord's giving, certainly. But his giving is not confined to the sacrament. What we need to focus on within the sacrament is our taking the love of God home with us, with a fresh awareness of that love. And that new awareness is the substance of the grace of the sacrament. Before reading another informative summary from Kiesling's *Paradigms of Sacramentality*, it will help to know that a 'paradigm' is an example which holds within it the essence of meaning, against which concepts can be examined and understood – a kind of fine example, a sure model.[28]

A final note on sacramentality
Kiesling writes, 'Baptism as incorporation into the Christian community is a paradigm of the sacramentality of all entrance into human community – family, city, nation, labour union, political party, school, bridge club. Confirmation is a model of all commitment to worthy human associations, causes and ideals. Penance is paradigmatic of all human reconciliation, whether

between members of families or of other communities, between proponents of opposing ideas of government.

'Further, anointing the sick is paradigmatic of the sacramentality of all care of the bodily and mentally ill, the economically and culturally deprived, the downtrodden, the rejected. Ordination is paradigmatic of the sacramentality of all human responsibility for the welfare of others, especially their common welfare, of all human leadership and government, whether in the narrow circle of the family or the wide circle of international life. The Eucharist is paradigmatic of the sacramentality of all self-sacrifice for others and for the causes of justice, love, freedom and truth. It is paradigmatic of the sacramentality of every meal which people share and of all human sharing, whether economic, cultural or spiritual. Marriage is paradigmatic of the sacramentality of every human encounter, every human friendship, every human love. It is paradigmatic too of the banalities of daily social life of every kind. The Word of God (in the sense of the Bible, the oral traditions behind it, and the words of God's spokespeople behind them) may be added to this list as paradigmatic of the sacramentality of all human speech and communication.'[29]

Unless we are aware of the sacramental nature of all reality and of the fact that our whole Christian life is worship, we cannot fully appreciate the constantly revealing mystery of the Incarnation, of the church and of the individual sacraments. What has been said up to now is that the world and all it contains is created out of the extravagant and unconditional love we call God. The breathtaking mystery of creation, past and present, is an incredibly beautiful sign of compassion, communicated to people, and reflecting the wisdom and loveliness of God. This, in itself, already makes the world holy and sacred. And then, this presence of the Spirit and the Word which were there from the beginning, as St John (and the sacraments) reminds us, is fleshed in Jesus Christ, consecrating again from within, a nature and an earthly reality that was sorely in need of salvation. 'Make ready for Christ,' shouts Thomas Merton, 'whose smile, like lightning, sets free the song of everlasting glory that now sleeps, in your paper flesh, like dynamite.'

The Sacrament of 'Simply Being'

The senses are thresholds of the soul

Out of the overwhelming intensity of divine love, God created the world in the first place for companionship. 'God is sheer joy', taught St Thomas Aquinas, 'and sheer joy demands company.' From that miraculous moment onwards, the world was permeated by God's indwelling love and energy. The Hebrew Scriptures make this quite clear. The pre-Christian contemplatives saw God's glory and felt God's presence in everyone and everything. In their silent wonder, the universal, indwelling love and meaning began to become more obvious. The very nature of creation, they began to understand, revealed the nature of God.

In the one person of Jesus, we find the unique and irrevocable meeting between creation's graced openness to divine fulfilment and God's creative and loving desire to achieve this intimacy. In him was completed and perfected the first longing of creation for God and God's own desire to fulfil that longing by becoming eternally united with humanity and creation. In him, the listening ear of a groaning and straining creation heard the divine music it was coded to hear from the beginning – the unceasingly uttered Word of a self-surrendering God. Christ revealed, once-for-all and in his own human self, the 'hidden agenda' of God's initial creation.

To live is holy

In his celebrated *Jubilee Letter* Pope John Paul II engaged with a theology of creation. As well as telling the mythical tale of humanity's fall from grace and a subsequent salvation, this rich understanding of revelation holds that creation and incarnation can also be read as the greatest love story, revealing all of us as being a delight to God, carefully fashioned in God's image. With or without a definitive 'fall', God longed for an intimate union with a human being and could not have been prevented from assuming the beautiful humanity of a man called Jesus. And it came to pass that the Word became flesh, and dwelt amongst us. All the hunches that a universal and divine energy ran through the still centre of everything, sustaining and nurturing growth and evolution of every kind, could now be completely believed. In Jesus, all the hints, suspicions and guesses about the God who moved in the inner heart of things, nourishing and caressing all forms of becoming, were, once-for-all, vindicated. From now on, the matter was beyond discussion – the unquestioned humanity of Jesus Christ was the living symbol and sacrament of God's assumption of creation as God's earthly mode of being.

The arrival of Jesus on the stage of life's evolution brought the drama of God and the world into another act. God's pure essence, which is love, is now guaranteed for ever, as being the source of the life of all living things. Those early Hebrew seers and prophets who, in their holy stillness, heard the faint, muffled rhythm of a deeper music, were not mistaken. Their pre-Christian souls were finely attuned to the divine score, long before it flowed across the world with its stunning beauty, in the symphony that was Jesus. There is a theological hint here for holding that to live is holy, that to simply be is blessed and that the condition of awareness is a true form of adoration. This prayer of awareness is coming from the gurus of the East and from the poets of the West, from the mystics of the past and the contemplatives of the present. It is as old as the hills and as new as a baby. It is not a special kind of awareness about a special kind of subject. It is any kind of true awareness about any part of created reality. That is why an intent and focused silence in the face of this amazing mystery is the main condition for hearing God's heartbeat in the cacophony of our lives. To simply be in the presence of the immediate commerce of life is the closest we can get to worship. The present moment is the real presence of God.

The Albuquerque Inn

At this point in my scribbling I pause to look around me. I stretch and breathe. My body is a little cramped but it feels good. I'm having a pint and a snack here in downtown Albuquerque. The Budweiser tastes weak; the cajun-style chicken is spicy and tasty. It is stiflingly hot outside; the air-conditioned inside is heaven. A small child's face is all crumpled up with loss and fear – she has just inadvertently burst her sister's red balloon. One grandparent chides her; the other smiles. There's music in the background – country and western songs from the sixties. A murmur of conversation. The telephone rings. A loud laugh draws attention to itself. Another car sweeps into the parking lot. Bright with smiles, energy, mutual adoration and jewellery, two young black people flow out of the car and dance into The Village Inn. The telephone rings again.

I come back to my thoughts. So this is it. If I'm right, here in front of me the true nature of God is being revealed. Right here and right now the paschal mystery is gradually unfolding in all its ordinariness and in all its glory. All I have to do is be present to it – really and truly present to it in a way that sees into the heart of things. This kind of worship is more than a superficial noticing; it is a becoming-one with what happens, and therefore a becoming-one with God. It is the practical implication of what our best spiritualities of incarnation keep reminding us about, namely, the presence of God everywhere – the God 'in whom we live and move and have our being'.

Here around the busy tables of The Village Inn, if we tune in to the amazing mystery of the most ordinary of daily happenings, multiplied by millions of times around the inns of the world, is the living-out of what we did around the Eucharistic table last Sunday. This was the celebration of what Jesus revealed in his life, death and resurrection, namely, that God is reaching to me in and between every beat of my heart, every breath I draw, every sound and movement around me, everything that happens, or ever happened, or ever will happen. So, as a human being and a Catholic Christian, what is this theological reflection saying to me then? It is simply saying – Wake up! Don't miss it! Be present to the miracle of the ordinary!

The full revelation of God in the full humanity of Jesus has signalled to the world that, by virtue of Jesus' solidarity with the rest of creation, the rest of creation, too, has the potential to reveal God. Jesus thought with a human mind, loved with a human heart and forgave with a human compassion.[30] It is to the extent that we are true in our human loving, authentic in our presence to our sisters and brothers, aware, compassionate and just in 'right relationship' with the fragile balances of the earth's resources, as Buddhists put it, that God becomes visible and tangible and knowable to us. Whenever, therefore, we are trying to be fully present to our own created essence, or to that of others, or to any created thing, even a drop of water or a grain of sand, that is when we aspire to intimacy with God.

To be is blessed
To be truly present, however, requires persistent awareness, attention, focus, the ability to stay with, to wonder at, to be lost in, to wake up to the holiness of the present moment. That is the reason for the prayer of quiet, for contemplation, for pursuing the mystical path. That is the reason for celebrating the sacraments, with all those natural elements that remind us of God's energy already flowing through all things. Without a deep awareness of God's healing presence in every aspect of time and space, from the beginning to the end, and in every split second and split atom in-between, our celebration of baptism and Eucharist can never be authentically sacramental.

In these pages I only want to indicate, with large brush strokes, the fundamental principles for holding that to 'simply be' is enough. We can say such a thing with faith and courage because, working backwards and forwards from the revelation that was

Jesus, we now know that God is always offering God's own self in every dimension of life. Every created moment and thing is a blessed sacrament of God's real presence. Whenever, for instance, we experience the heartfelt feelings of anyone, we are experiencing God. Whenever we truly love anybody, we somehow redeem that person forever, because our love is, as St Augustine said, divine love incarnate. When we forgive somebody, that person is forgiven by God. This is so amazing that most people dismiss it as untrue. It is too simple and too profound. To love anyone truly is to be another Christ, to be God incarnate.

There are not two separate ways of loving. There is not another 'higher' level of being called 'holy'. To believe otherwise is to be guilty of the dualism we considered earlier, to deny the meaning of the Incarnation. We want signs and wonders, oblivious to the miracles around us every day. We want priests and scapegoats as 'in-betweens', between ourselves and God and between ourselves and sin and between ourselves and ourselves. We would rather live in a two-tier world, misunderstanding the whole point of the Incarnation, pandering to magic and superstition in our dualistic devotions, seeing 'ordinary' life as 'merely' secular and always hankering after the 'sacred' people, sacred places and sacred things as though God was somehow more fully there. It is a fruitless search because the divine beauty is already lying in abundance at the fingertips of our hearts and bodies. In Daniel Ladinsky's *I Heard God Laughing*, the fourteenth-century Persian Sufi poet Hafiz had his own unique way of putting it:

> *One regret, dear world,*
> *That I am determined not to have*
> *When I am lying on my deathbed*
> *Is that*
> *I did not kiss you enough.*[31]

Only one love
We forget that the world is the body of God, that, as the poets remember, eternity is caught in the most commonplace moment, infinity in a passing gesture and divinity in every aspiration of the

human heart. Without the fact of the enfleshing of the Word, no poet or mystic could hold, with absolute certainty, what the Hebrew authors glimpsed – that every drop of water, every grain of sand, every leaf, every feeling are all small sacraments of divinity. So important and holy is the 'being' of things, the 'isness' and 'inscape' of things, the life-breath of any creature, the heartbeat of the tiniest insect, that to become one with it, is to become one with God.

We listen to the anonymous mystic author of *The Cloud of Unknowing*: 'If you look at God in the perspective of eternity,' the author writes, 'there is no name you can give him – nor is there any experience or understanding – which is more fitting than that which is contained in the blind and lovely beholding of the word *is*.' Above all, when we struggle to love as truly as we can, then, especially, is when we are held in mystery. (Mystery being, not an impossible puzzle, but the context and unfathomable backdrop, the infinite horizon to all our human searching and loving.) So when we stop thinking distracting thoughts, when we are attentive to the present moment and to all that is going on all around us, when we trust in the 'now', letting go of everything that is not in that 'now', then, to my mind, we are sensing the liberating reality of God.

The mystics describe this kind of attention as something like the way people in love gaze in silence at each other and are privileged to enter some reserved inner sanctum, out of bounds to all but the lover. When people are gifted with this mutual loving, there is a deeper mystery present. The revelation of the Incarnation is not about a third element in this relationship, as though God's love was another dimension to be included in the equation. Any form of human loving is impossible without God; the more purified and authentic it is, the more completely it can be identified with divine love.

It was, after all, in Jesus' sensitive human presence to his relationships, in his attentive struggles with them, in all his human loveableness, in his attractiveness as a deeply caring human being, that God's essence was revealed, and that the church community was founded. It was in the warmth of his smile, the look in his eyes, the magnetism of his awareness of people's guilt and fear, that God wished to be accessible to the world. For the Christian, there is no other way to experience and worship the sacred, human heart of God (1 Jn 1:1–6).

Given our human condition, in time and space, and given God's assumption of that finite condition as the full and sufficient medium of continuing revelation, there is nothing any more concerning the reality of God in Jesus that lies outside of humanity, of human experience, of the totality of creation. *To simply be* is to be able, like the hub of a wheel, to hold all the vibrant spokes together. *To simply be* is to be attentive enough to the shifting surfaces of life, like a human spirit level, bringing into right relationship what is out of true. *To simply be* is to be attuned enough to one's inner, divine harmony, so as to be a tuning fork, bringing discordant voices into true pitch. *To simply be* is to be a map, a compass, for those who are lost.

The purpose of silence in our lives, of non-verbal ways of being present to ourselves and to others, is simply and precisely to heighten our awareness of the subtleties of life – those nooks and crannies in the labyrinths of our daily work and play – those same nooks and crannies in which God is waiting to be found. *To simply be*, above all, is to be in our bodies. Because of God's initial desire, fall or no fall, as we saw, to assume created humanity, to be transformed into flesh, God's pure being is now available in human bodies. It seems as though there is a divine obsession with the physical. From God's delight in assuming the small body of a baby, to Jesus' amazing plan to become the very flesh and bone of human beings through our eating and drinking of his own body in the medium of bread and wine, it is no wonder that, in a more enlightened orthodoxy, the body and all its spiritual and sexual powers is seen as the very tabernacle of divinity.

Sacraments of simply being

To simply be before God and the world will draw us into the need for some kind of public, liturgical expression or celebration of our experiences. One sentence from the library of Karl Rahner's writings has led me into exhilarating ways of re-envisioning liturgy – *sacraments celebrate what is already there*. Again, it is all about being attentive to the way things are. Without this awareness, we are back in a dualistic mode where the sacred and the secular belong to different worlds.

Because of our congenital forgetfulness and existential blindness, the role of liturgy in our faith-lives is paramount. For the Christian, that goes without saying. But before liturgical celebration in church can make any Christian sense, the liturgy of the world must first be entered into. The Irish poet Patrick Kavanagh finds God 'in the bits and pieces' of daily life. In *The Liturgy of the World: Karl Rahner's Theology of Worship*, we see that Rahner is convinced that 'we will be only able to recognise the presence of the absolute mystery in the liturgy if we first recognise its abiding presence throughout our whole lives and in all the world'. Writing about this loving mystery that is easily ignored or overlooked because of its hidden nature, he feels the need to 'dig it out, so to speak, from under the refuse of the ordinary business of life'.[32] This detection of the quiet gift of the abundant life, waiting to be discovered in the shadow and light of each night and day, is the work of the mystic.

Every time we celebrate the saving mysteries of creation and incarnation, we remember and reactivate God's initial creative work and God's subsequent and continuing redemptive action in the past and present. We affirm, celebrate and intensify the constant presence of grace in our midst from the fiery beginning of our cosmic story, through the fourteen billion years of evolution, into the current shoving, straining and groaning of the world, forever painfully giving birth to new beauty. In the prologue to his Gospel, John reminds us that Love has always been incarnate. This story of the continual unfolding of God's love for us is true of everything from the personal details of our own painful, joyful, inner and outer journeys to the currently stunning revelations of the mysteries of the cosmos.

Most of our best theologians, poets and mystics throughout the centuries of Christianity are excitingly clear about a theology of creation, of nature and grace, and about the principles of sacramentality. Once we make the paradigm shift from a dualistic, 'redemption-only' interpretation of incarnation, into a wider and more creation-centred, love-inspired understanding of salvation and revelation, then the old doctrines of our faith become pregnant with new possibilities, opening out before us like a freshly-furrowed field waiting for the new grain of our transformed consciousness.

Evolution and the Holy Spirit

God in the heart of the cosmos and the cosmos of the heart

We were on our way back home after Benediction one bright night, many decades ago, my mother and myself, when she reached for my hand and suddenly stopped walking. 'Look up,' she said, 'look up and listen.' I still remember it as a mystical moment. Something inside us stands in amazement under the sky at night. There is a curious bond, a sacramental intimacy, between the universe of our heart and the heart of our universe, as they spin around each other in a web of wonder.

At the opening of the 2012 Paralympic Games in London, Stephen Hawking said: 'Look up at the stars, not down at your feet. Try to make sense of what you see, and wonder about what makes the universe exist. Be curious.'

Cosmic connection of the heart

There was a hidden hint of theology and cosmology in my mother's remark that winter's evening. We sense the cosmic connections by heart. Pentecost is taking place whenever invisible mystery is becoming visible, whenever the unknown becomes accessible, when incarnate divinity lights up our soul. It is taking place wherever life moves on towards its final goal, wherever the evolving universe is unfolding towards its ultimate realisation, because it is the Holy Spirit that is facilitating and enabling that compelling attraction.

Theologian Karl Rahner deplores the poverty of our theology of the Spirit, which deeply misunderstands its universal significance and primal potency. He reminds us that the Holy Spirit is revealed as the divine power in the deepest heart of each person and of this earthly world. This power is the graced centre of creation, divinely imbued with the evolving potential to reach its completion when God will be 'all in all'.

'And here the earth,' he writes, 'behind her continual development in space and time, sinks her root into the power of the all-mighty God ... his Spirit has already begun to transform the world into himself ... the new creation has already started, the new power of a transfigured earth is already being formed from the world's innermost heart.'[33]

Priest and scientist Teilhard de Chardin had a unique insight into the interweaving of the evolving planet and the work of the Holy Spirit. His Pentecost moment came when he was inspired to recognise that all becoming and developing in an expanding universe is animated by the divine drive of the Holy Spirit. 'For Teilhard', wrote Professor Ursula King in her *Pierre Teilhard de Chardin*, 'the heart of God is found at the heart of the world, and the living, natural world is shot through with the presence of the divine, with what he eventually was to call "the divine milieu".'[34]

By this he meant that our universe is a christified one, infused by the divine presence in all that happens. The cosmic Christ is the centre of the universe, of humanity, of each person, and 'at the heart of the tiniest atom'. For him faith consecrates the world. It sees the 'divine fire' hidden in the body of the world. 'Oh the beauty of Spirit', he exclaimed, 'as it rises up adorned with all the riches of the earth.' His faith was incarnational, sacramental and Christ-centred.[35]

Our mystics, physicists and theologians are combining to provide images of a vibrant, utterly free and unpredictable Holy Spirit that transcends our current and misleadingly limited understanding of its dynamic presence. St Augustine saw the totality of creation as a huge sponge immersed in a boundless sea, each tiny particle of it saturated with the ocean of the Spirit. 'I set before the sight of my soul', he wrote, 'the whole creation (stars, earth, air and mortal creatures); yea, and whatever we do not see ... And thee, O Lord, I imagined on every part environing and pervading it, though in every way infinite.'

'Groaning with the world,' writes Professor Elizabeth Johnson in *Quest for the Living God*, 'delighting in its advance, keeping faith with its failures, energising it graciously from within, the Creator Spirit is with all creatures in their finitude and death, holding them in redemptive love and drawing them into an unforeseeable future in the divine communion.'[36]

Diarmuid O'Murchu's *In the Beginning was the Spirit* liberates the Holy Spirit from our deadly doctrinal descriptions. 'Spirit', he writes, 'is the wellspring of all possibility, the restless pulsation of every movement of creation and of every desire in the human heart. It is the power of becoming that awakens every stir of imagination, wisdom and creativity.'[37]

We strive for something more because deep in our hearts the Spirit lures us to do so. The restlessness within is a divine one, the fruit of the enlivening, energising and empowering Spirit, the same Spirit that blows where it wills and that never ceases to amaze and surprise us. '[It] belongs primarily', he writes, 'to the world itself, and not to any church or religion. And it is present with a cosmic passion and a personal intimacy.'[38]

One could say that the Pentecost Spirit lives in the core of the natural universe, firing and energising its inevitable evolution, tenderly holding all creatures in their finitude and death, and urging and drawing the world forward toward an unfathomable future. In his *Redemptoris Missio* (1990), Pope John Paul II explains that 'the presence and activity of the Spirit are universal, limited neither by space or time ... affecting society and history, peoples, cultures and religions.'

The dynamism of the Holy Spirit pulses through the Church, through humanity and through the evolving world. Pentecost reminds us that the Holy Spirit is a power at work in a continually renewed universe, and is present in the innermost mystery of all things. Grace and science come together to offer a fuller picture of what is true: that God's love is embodied in all humanity, and in the evolving world itself. The light that appears in Jesus is none other than that which had already shone forth in creation.

Maybe my mother's silent wonder on that winter's evening in 1947 arose from a sense of being held by a Spirit of connecting, belonging and intimacy. 'At such moments', writes O'Murchu, 'we know instinctively and intuitively that all is one, that relationship defines the very core of life itself.'[39] And then we kneel with Pierre Teilhard in utterly personal and universal adoration. 'I love you', he prayed in his lyrical *Hymn of the Universe*, 'for the extensions to your body and soul in the farthest corners of creation through grace, through life, through matter. Lord Jesus, you who are as gentle as the human heart, as fiery as the forces of nature, as intimate as life itself, you in whom I can melt away and with whom I must have mastery and freedom: I love you as the world, as *this* world which has captivated my heart; and it is you, I now realise, that people, even those who do not believe, sense and see through the magic immensities of the cosmos.'[40]

Fire in the depths of the earth

Breaking through into new vistas is an essential dimension of a renewed and necessary Pentecost today. The Mass Collect of the feast implores God to 'fill now once more the hearts of believers', encouraging us to expand the horizons of our hearts and minds. Such a Pentecost, for theologian Rahner, is a vital 'hour of courageous vision' in the history of the Church, when the Holy Spirit weaves new patterns out of the 'interrelatedness of Creation and Incarnation'.

A central path, for him, towards that expansion of the restless heart's horizon, concerns the currently popular question about the divine intention for the Incarnation – did Jesus come to atone for the sin of Adam and Eve, or would he have come anyway?

Beyond doctrinal debate, this is a crucial question with implications for every aspect of our lives – personal and universal. Is there a theology, people ask, other than one based on a fall/redemption supposition, that tells a different story – a story of original grace and beauty rather than of original sin?

By way of reply, theologians point to two schools of theology that are central to our present reflection. One is the familiar sin/redemption model with its basic themes of reparation and sacrifice. The other is a theology of nature and grace. Creation, our earth, our bodies, our death, all we mean by the 'natural', 'the secular', are not the unfortunate results of what Blessed John Henry Newman called 'some terrible aboriginal calamity'. On the contrary, they are all already graced, and carefully fashioned in the divine image.

But if there was no 'single original fall', people ask, why then are we so sinful, so destructive, so evil? This is a huge and perennial question. Philosophers and great thinkers continually struggle with it. Every culture and religion have their own stories. Many Christian theologians reply that the act of Creation in the very first place – involving time, space and free will – carries within it the need for redemption. Salvation is implicit in Creation itself. To be human is to be wounded from the start, to be in need of completion. We need clear minds and attentive hearts, and humble study and discussion, to contemplate these observations so as to begin to understand more of the mystery.

Love is what completes us

'We were already saved', writes Richard Rohr OFM, 'by the gaze from the manger.' The terrible death on the Cross is not about an atonement demanded by a punitive Father for one early original sin of disobedience; it reveals, rather, the astonishing love of God for a broken humanity, healing it and charting its course towards its blessed destiny.

An orthodox theology of Creation holds that God, right from the beginning, desired to become human simply because, as St Thomas Aquinas put it, God's infinite love needed to express itself outside itself (*bonum est diffusivum sui*) – first in Creation, then finally and fully revealed in Incarnation. And by virtue of solidarity and derivation, this love is embodied to a greater or lesser degree in all of us and in the evolving world itself.

Being human does not mean being banished, fallen, cursed – a *massa damnata* as St Augustine put it – as if God's original dream for us was, at some stage, radically destroyed. Terrible things happen when mythical truth is confused with historical truth. Paradise was not lost in the past; Adam and Eve never existed on this planet; the Creator's original blueprint was never destroyed by an actual 'fall'.

If all of this is true – that the essential face of Creation, as we have it, has always carried the tender look of love rather than the sinister shape of sin – then other intrinsically connected issues to do with the vibrancy of faith will need careful revision and development.

Here is one topical example. People sense that we're at a very significant threshold in history where two pivotal stories meet – the love story revealed in the orthodox theology of nature and grace, and the amazing story revealed in the scientific explorations of a painfully evolving and utterly wonderful world.

These stories do not have to collide with each other: if anything they embrace each other, offering a fuller picture of what is beautiful and true. They both speak of a fundamental connectedness in our origins, evolution and destiny. The emerging cosmology, often called the New Universe Story, can be seen as validating the rich theological (but mostly neglected) vision which has always been at the heart of true Christianity.

A new consciousness of the bigger picture is called for, a clearer insight into the intrinsic connection between Creation and Incarnation, into the deepening conversation between the mystic and the physicist. A fundamental concept is that we all flow from one source; some will call it the process of evolution, others the work of the Holy Spirit.

In *Field of Compassion*, Judy Cannato writes, 'There is a single Creator of the entire cosmos, a Creator who remains present to every part of the cosmos, sustaining and empowering its ongoing life and development. This same Creator will bring the whole movement of evolutionary Creation to completion.'[41] The original divine design in our evolving world is revealed in incarnation, to be fulfilled in the 'Omega' of Christian Revelation (Rev 3; 4).

Evolution, you could say, is intrinsic to incarnation. It is how Creation, already containing the divine seed, has prepared the necessary ground – the human era – for the birthing of God. There is a sense in which Creation is the beginning of incarnation, 'the first Bible', as Aquinas put it.

Pentecost reminds us that God's fire already burns in the darkest depths of the living earth. Ultimately, for the Christian, the Holy Spirit is present as the innermost mystery of all things, and may be understood as the invisible power at work in a continually evolving universe, until God be 'all in all'. There is now no longer a destructive dualism between the things of God and the things of earth. 'When we want both the God of infinity and the spirit within the familiar (evolving) universe, as it is, and as it shall become, there is one path to both,' writes Rahner.

The recovery of a theology of nature and grace, now enriched by the emerging insights of the new cosmology, will have profound implications for many Christian teachings, for our understanding of sacrament, for pastoral ministry, for the religion/science debate and for a new evangelising of young and old. It will help, above all, to shift our self-image as fallen failures, complicit somehow in the death of Jesus, to an awareness of our role as vital co-creators with God of a steadily developing, ever-evolving universe. We are not guilty exiles on a fallen earth – we are the beloved bearers of Her divine dream.

Song of the Seals – a personal reflection by Margaret Siberry
Out on the sandbank across from the Holy Island of Lindisfarne the seals are calling to each other in their haunting evening chorus. Their strange, primordial sound is entrancing, stilling. Carried on the late evening breeze over the narrow stretch of water, their song wafts over me, gradually drawing me in, as if enveloping me in their melody, their mysterious telling of their story – our story. Today is the summer solstice and here in the northern hemisphere the earth is enjoying its longest day before it gently turns away from the sun on its tilting axis and journeys onward through the year. The song of the seals this evening seems to come from a place of deep knowing and I am quietened, drawn into a soul-space that awakens a sense of immense presence – a presence that feels almost tangible in sea and sky and rock. It is as if they are calling me to

really see what is before me. I wait and gaze and listen, savouring the caress of the breeze. It is as if my senses have a heightened awareness, as if creation itself is calling out to be noticed, to be recognised in this moment and I'm left with a profound and overwhelming sense of awe. The feeling is powerful and I don't want to move. There is a growing sense of deep belonging, of connection, of being immersed within the wonder and mystery of all that surrounds me. It is a moment of startling clarity.

I'm sure that we have all experienced moments when we have been moved by nature, when something inside has stirred and we are moved to a deeper place of recognition. We began this chapter with such a fleeting, powerful experience. Those moments touch the most profound truth, that creation itself is the unfolding story of how our creator God reveals the God-self. The hope in this reflection is to offer a very brief exploration of how entering this story offers another lens through which to glimpse the presence of God in every aspect of life.

In the last fifty years scientific discoveries about the origin and emergence of the universe have fired the imagination and opened up new windows on the love and meaning at the heart of creation. This 'New Universe Story', as it is called, discloses and celebrates that the universe itself is the unfolding of God's story, that our Creator chooses to communicate the God-self in the energy bursting forth at the beginning of time and in all that has emerged and is still unfolding. This is the fundamental understanding of a theology of nature and grace – that creation itself is sacred, carries the imprint of God and is itself the first scripture. Viewed in this way, the very essence of the ongoing creation story holds the key to entering the wonder of being human. If we open ourselves to the dynamics that permeate the cosmos, we open ourselves to the mystery of who we are in God.

To glimpse the magnificence and complexity at the heart of the cosmos is to be awakened to the expansiveness and beneficence of a wildly generative God. Our small, confining images fall away and we enter into the wonder of our Creator's unimaginable generosity – expressed in galaxies, stars, rocks and oceans, birds and fish, animals and insects, you and me. And, all is held in dynamic relationship through the fundamental principles and laws of physics that scientists are still discovering and exploring. Through science we are reclaiming the ancient wisdom that our early ancestors intuitively lived – the interconnectedness and interdependence of all life. The true nature of God is revealed within a wondrous and complex universe and in the moments when we glimpse this, something deep in us is touched. Reverence, awe and gratitude are the only responses. These rare but graced moments of tuning in don't happen often but when they do our world view is transformed. We know intuitively, at a profound level, that there is no separation between the sacred and the material, all is one.

From the moment when the first astronauts viewed planet Earth from space, human consciousness was changed for ever. Their unexpected, poetic language spoke of the beauty and fragility of this tiny blue sphere floating in space, and holding all that humanity has known, experienced and cherished. They sensed a deep relationship and wanted to protect their tiny and vulnerable planet home. In the debriefs and interviews on their return, all of them spoke as if planet Earth was a living being, giving credence to the emerging Gaia theory that understands our planet as a living organism with its own self-organising dynamics. The illusion that we can stand 'outside' creation was replaced with a deepening awareness that we are merely the latest expressions of the universe's ever more complex unfolding story.

Interpreting these discoveries through the lens of the Christian story redefines our image of God and of the universe we inhabit. The 'Big Bang', or as cosmologist Brian Swimme prefers, the 'silent flaring forth', reveals a God whose love is so immense that it cannot be contained, but, in time and space, bursts forth in a quantum of energy, whose story is told in the birth and death of stars, the forming of galaxies, the intricate orbit of planets, the elements that eventually generate matter, life on planet Earth, humans. We are indeed stardust and we are made to shine as brightly as the stars.

'In the beginning was the Word' wrote St John, expressing the fundamental truth about our origin. The surge of curiosity and excitement when the news broke that the great Hadron Collider was working, that scientists might actually find the 'God particle', that the question of our origin might now be discovered, was headline news on all channels. Scientists are forever fascinated by this question, and are drawn to explore the cosmos with ever more refined technology, searching for evidence of life on distant planets and seeking to explain dark matter, black holes and the possibility that we live in a multiverse rather than a universe. These are innovative times that invite us to let our imagination soar and enter into new depths of meaning, new insights into the sacredness of the universe itself.

Three laws

The more we understand the dynamics that are at the heart of the universe the more we understand the heart of God. In his *Dream of the Earth* theologian and physicist Fr Thomas Berry describes three fundamental laws of the universe – differentiation, subjectivity and communion – that describe the relationship in which all creation is held and that reveal God's presence within all and within us.[42] If we take even the smallest time to contemplate the immense variety of life forms – plants, creatures, landscapes, seas and stars – all the infinite possibilities of life as we know it, we discover that each life form is uniquely created and each plays its part in the intricate web of life. Put simply, differentiation is the way of the universe and is the hallmark of a generative Creator who delights in giving self-expression ever more imaginatively, abundantly, and with wild generosity

Second, every unique element within creation has its own intrinsic presence – 'inscape' – as Gerard Manley Hopkins describes it. Sadly it has become customary, since the Industrial Revolution especially, to regard elements within creation in a utilitarian way as if they were only objects, commodities to be used by humans as befits our need or want. In this way, Berry would argue, we have lost a sense of wonder and recognition that each created thing carries its own unique interiority, subjectivity and beauty, and this more accurate understanding is to recognise that we are all subjects, each creature tasked with flagging forth the divine in a way that no other can.

Though unique, every aspect of life as we know it is held in an intricate web of interdependent relationships, a myriad of ecosystems that are bound together in what Berry calls a 'communion'. This third, fundamental law of how the universe organises itself, works its way in, and through us too, and calls us to live in the same kind of communion. This is our nature, who we are in essence and it is what we remember every time we celebrate the Eucharist. The challenge is to live true to our essence, to fulfil our part as co-creators, celebrating and enhancing the communion of all life.[43]

Brian Swimme suggests that one of the ways to enter into the universe story and to experience being within rather than apart from creation is to go out at sunrise or sunset and imagine our planet-home slowly turning, rather than holding on to the concept that the sun 'goes down'. Sunrise and sunset are gateways, breakthrough moments into a different vision that disclose reality and touch another level of being. The Sun, our star with such a mass that it pulls our tiny planet Earth in its orbit, and without which there would be no life, is unparalleled in its generosity. Scientists studying the dynamics of the Sun realise that it is dying. Every second the Sun transforms four million tons of itself into light, providing the energy without which life on Earth could not flourish – a cosmological sacrifice that has been happening since the beginning, and an image of the paschal mystery.

In his *Hidden Heart of the Cosmos* Swimme's telling of the story paints a vivid picture: 'The sun converts itself into a flow of energy that photosynthesis changes into plants that are consumed by animals. So for four million years,[44] humans have been feasting on the sun's energy stored in wheat or maize or deer as the sun dies and is reborn as the vitality of the earth. And those solar flares are in fact the very power of the vast human enterprise. And every child needs to learn the simple truth; she is the energy of the *sun*. And we adults should organise things so that her face shines with the same radiant joy.

'In the new millennium the sun's extravagant bestowal of energy can be regarded as a spectacular manifestation of an underlying impulse pervading the universe. In the star this impulse reveals itself in the ongoing giveaway of energy. In the human heart it is felt as the urge to devote one's life to the well-being of the larger community.'[45]

Another suggestion from Swimme is to lie on your back in a quiet place in the open air and be mindful of the gravitational pull of the earth and imagine looking down into deep space rather than up as we nearly always conceptualise it. The point here is to feel the attraction, the basic law that keeps our planet in its orbit and everything on it from floating off into space. The allurement we feel within us, the way we are drawn to follow our attractions, mirrors the gravitational pull at the heart of the universe. It is the dynamic of the ongoing story of the universe, the story of God's creative energy working within us too. When we follow our allurement we are following God's dream for us, we are participating in the creative process.

To sit and ponder the laws and dynamics of the universe in this way evokes wonder, celebration and gratitude. It offers an entirely different image of God – a God of *inscendence* rather than *transcendence* within all life and each life – a sacramental vision. The gift of scientific adventure is the capacity to see and understand what was here all along. That capacity is already a gift of imagination, but Swimme, Berry and others would argue that science is now entering its wisdom phase when what is at stake is the *meaning* of scientific discovery for the ongoing cosmological adventure. When we interpret the scientific adventure within the Christian story, that meaning becomes clearer, the 'sacramental imagination' is ignited and opens us to the deeper meaning within all life. There is an incredible adventure before us as we, too, come into our wisdom stage and become the mystics that the world needs.

The Artist makes the Invisible Visible

Art as window and mirror on the world, as prism of mystery incarnate

To see God in the everyday, the divine in the worldly, the transcendent in the ordinary – that is what this chapter is about (indeed what the whole book is about) but here we call on the artist to help us achieve this kind of seeing. The emphasis will be on the artist as painter, and as painter of secular pictures. How do the works of the famous artists of our time, like 'secular parables', speak about God? Even where the artist has no theological interests, how, in the light of faith, does the work empower the viewer to see things differently, especially, for the Christian, something of the numinous, of the face of God?

In his *Letter to Artists* (1999) Pope John Paul II wrote: 'None can sense more deeply than you artists, ingenious creators of beauty that you are, something of the pathos with which God at the dawn of creation looked upon the work of his hands. A glimmer of that feeling has shone so often in your eyes when – like the artists of every age – captivated by the hidden power of sounds and words, colours and shapes, you have admired the work of your inspiration, sensing in it some echo of the mystery of creation with which God, the sole creator of all things, has wished to associate you ... With loving regard, the divine Artist passes on to the human artist a spark of his own surpassing wisdom, calling him to share in his creative power.'

The Pope went on to emphasise that 'every genuine art form in its way – from writers, painters, sculptors, poets, film-makers, playwrights, composers, architects, musicians, actors – is a path to the innermost reality of man and of the world ... That is why the Gospel fullness of truth was bound from the beginning to stir the interest of artists, who by their very nature are alert to every epiphany of the inner beauty of things.' Each work of art', he said, 'which explores the everyday, the darkest depth of the soul [is] an appeal to mystery, [a] genuine source of theology, [a] moment of grace ... a kind of sacrament making present the Incarnation in one or other of its aspects.'

Small Incarnations

Because God became incarnate in creation and in humanity, it is in these time-and-space realities that we find a way into Mystery. In this chapter I rely chiefly on T.J. Gorringe's acclaimed *Earthly Visions: Theology and the Challenges of Art*. Gorringe argues that great art can function as a 'secular parable' leading viewers to reflect on the reality and presence of God in the world. He does this by helping them 'to read each painting theologically, and, in fact, to see everything differently'. He writes from the context of a theology of creation, a spirituality of nature and grace.

He refers to many theologians, especially Karl Barth, who wrote that creation is good because it is the product of divine joy. 'It is the goodness of God that takes shape in it, and God's good pleasure is both the foundation and the end of creation ... There is no such thing as merely secular history.' The secular is not 'godless'. The truly secular is compatible with the sacred if not, indeed, the sacred 'per se', he wrote.[46]

It is not so much about inserting or including a hint of heaven that makes a painting, a dance, a piece of music 'religious'; it is in capturing the utter truth of anything earthly that, unknowingly, provides an experience of the divine. John Ruskin wrote that 'the artist is gifted with the ability to see and represent in his work the divine origin of all created works, and so to be able to direct the less perceptive to see it for themselves.'

In a lecture Christian artist Wendy Beckett spoke about Sally Warner, an American contemporary painter, who draws trees, brushwood, stone – which are luminous with God. She also talked about William Bailey, another, older American, who paints jugs and kitchen vessels and a wooden table with a sacramental strength that is overpowering. 'Avigdor Arikha', Beckett went on, 'an Israeli, can show us a bare wall, a broom, bottles, young women, rooms and stairways, or scattered shoes and socks, and the viewer is seized by the wonder of what is seen. No attempt is made to glorify the shoes and socks. But the artist has seen their simple quiddity, their truth to their own nature, their materiality, as purely beautiful.'

Whenever art captures the core being, the truth, the 'isness' or interiority of anything, there too is a moment of divine revelation. It is only in the authenticity of 'what is' that the face of the Christian God can be glimpsed. The radical role of the artist is to keep reminding us of that. Where the Church fails, the artist is often the one who brings a graced seeing into a superficial looking, a blessed hearing into a shallow listening.

Revealing the essence

Philosopher Merleau-Ponty believed that the most profound artists may have something to say about the grace, in which, according to the Christian tradition, the whole of reality is suspended, sustained, 'as a singer sustains her song, but which it requires revelation to become aware of – to *see*'. The angel has to come to stir the water before we can wake to incarnation, to put fire to the stubble so as to glimpse the infinite horizon.[47]

In his 'Painting and the Absence of Grace' Oliver Soskice has this to say about the artist's efforts to draw out the essence of something, to touch the mystery of life itself. This, for the Christian, is the exploration into God. Soskice writes: 'Inexpressibly *other* from the nature of every being, existence is received as the unreachable beckoning horizon within stones, the sky, brickwork rained upon, daylight, pools of reflecting water, apples in a bowl. A painter may spend a lifetime trying to translate this strange, innermost utterance of visible things.'[48]

Cézanne became a regular church-goer towards the end of his life. He did not attempt religious themes in his paintings. He concentrated upon landscape and still life. Yet, Gorringe tells us, through his delight in the colour and shapes of the world, he delights also in God. For the Russian painter Kandinsky, Cézanne saw the inner life in everything, and believed that colours came from the roots of the world – he tried to find colours for grace. Van Gogh said he could not look at a picture by Rembrandt without believing in God.

While much has been written about the gift of beauty provided by the vision and work of artists such as Turner and Monet, their contribution has been more profoundly described as their cleansing of 'the doors of perception'. 'They have sensed', according to Gorringe, 'and help others to see, the glory patent in the ordinary, the transfiguration of the real … Most of the time we are unable to see that; part of the abiding appeal of landscape painting is that, at its best, it opens our eyes, as the eyes of the disciples were opened, so see the ordinary in a completely different way.'[49]

'Art', says Rowan Williams in his *Grace and Necessity*, 'in one sense dispossesses us of our habitual perception and restores a reality, a dimension that necessarily escapes our conceptuality and our control. It makes the world strange.' With reference to still-life paintings Gorringe argues that since they emerged at the end of the fifteenth century they have set before us a vision of creation as benefit, as grace, charged with grandeur, which invests our ordinary mundane lives, mediating the presence of God.[50]

'Painters', Gorringe writes, 'are those who see such signs and help the rest of us to see them. In "The Bright Field" the poet R. S. Thomas dwells on one of his favourite images; when the sun streaming through clouds, picks out one field among many. Like the poet, the painter renders visible as a phenomenon what no one had ever seen before, because he or she manages, being the first to do that every time, to resist the given enough to get it to show itself.'[51]

It is not by holy additions to 'secular' art that the numinous is expressed; it is by one's understanding of the secular in the first place. For example, as Gorringe so succinctly puts it, 'precisely because the creaturely world is, for the Christian, the creation of God, and precisely because, in theological terms, creation is the expression of grace, it has also, as such, and as Barth put it, 'its own lights and truths, and therefore, its own speech and words' to reveal its divine origin and destiny. The theatre, the gallery, the poetry-reading room have become the places of pilgrimage, the second book of revelation'.[52]

The various faces and interpretations of reality in the work of an artist, are, for the Christian, privileged windows into the beyond and the within, incarnate epiphanies of the divine. Secular parables then, auditory and visible ones, are part of God's revelation. They are this without losing their secular character or undergoing any inner transformation. 'The aim of the artist', writes Flannery O'Connor, 'is to render the highest possible justice to the visible universe … The artist penetrates the concrete world in order to find at its depths the image of its source, the image of ultimate reality.'

Hidden Meanings

In his book, *Earthly Visions*, Gorringe examines representative secular paintings of the most significant types, explaining how each one expresses something of a deeper, divine creator. He makes us look again at the hidden meanings of the secular. To help us in this graced quest of looking, seeing and recognising we have the wonderful theology of a Barth, a Tillich, a Rahner, an Aquinas to transform our consciousness when we pause to gaze at the beauty of a Boticelli, a Rothko, a Monet, a Turner, and when we linger to listen to a Mozart, a Schubert, a Vivaldi, a Verdi.

'To read secular art theologically', writes Gorringe at the end of his book, 'is to insist on questioning, on the dimension of depth, to resist premature efforts at closure of meaning. It is to situate art within such a tradition of questioning and meaning … It invites us to reflect more deeply on the mystery of existence … The crowds that throng to art galleries and exhibitions go, I suspect, not just in search of a meaning they do not find elsewhere in society, and which the church no longer conveys for them, but because they are interested in these rumours (of angels everywhere), because there are parables which still speak of the elusive but pressing mystery of the world ... The whole world is, as George Macleod liked to say of Iona, "a thin place". All that is, is the product of the divine Word, which is to say the divine imagination and joy, loving reality into being.'[53]

Roman Catholic philosophers Bernard Lonergan and Jacques Maritain are quoted in *The Critical Spirit*, emphasising, in their references to the process of education, the necessary role of a free exploration of art and of the emotions. Our presence to great art, they said, is what keeps our lives and the world in tune with God. Lonergan claimed that 'the life we are living is a product of artistic creation' and that it is on the artistic, symbolic level that we live our full range of humanity, discovering that we can become 'emergent, ecstatic, standing out ... in originating freedom'.[54]

Maritain consistently emphasised the urgent need for the student in all of us to be nourished in the banquet of art so as to guide people 'in the evolving dynamism through which they shape themselves as human beings', bringing to realisation what is already God-given in their nature. In *Education at the Crossroads*, he warns against squeezing the soul into the limited shapes we teach. He pleads for a respect, through art, for 'the sense of each one's innermost essence and internal resources, a sort of loving attention to their mysterious identity that no techniques can reach'.[55]

True art, Bishop Richard Harries believes, always has a spiritual dimension. 'Yet', he writes in his *Art and the Beauty of God*, 'if religion tries to turn it into propaganda, the spiritual could slip away. Works of art inescapably witness, by their truth and beauty, to their fount and origin in God himself. Yet religion, always in danger of being corrupted and corrupting, does not have this art at its beck and call. It cannot use it for its own ends.'[56]

Nevertheless, there is a very neglected theology of nature and grace, of a sacramental vision, of 'the catholic imagination' that provides a wonderful context for all we have been considering in this chapter. It is orthodox, traditional, mystical and espoused by theologians from the very beginning, and is once again making a welcome and timely appearance.

The artist may or may not be a religious believer. From an artistic point of view that does not affect the spirituality of the created work. What does matter is a kind of ruthless authenticity and truthfulness, what Harries calls a 'fundamental seriousness, a fierce artistic integrity'. Without this it will be impossible to find the beauty in the damaged, the truth in the twisted, the invisible in the visible, the grace in everything.

Sin is Blind to Beauty

It has no imagination; it denies incarnation

By this stage there must be many readers wondering about the place and reality of sin, personal and original, in such an overview of revelation, and about its consequent implications for the redemptive role of the church today. Most of us are well-versed in the catechism definitions and distinctions of sin, and of the huge part this whole doctrine plays in our faith and in our lives. The following ideas are offered in the light of a theology of nature and grace, and of its sister, a spirituality of the human heart.

Original Sin and Original Blessing

As with personal sin, original sin has worked its way into the heart of our faith, our theology and our daily Christian lives. Millions of Catholics still take the Adam and Eve story quite literally, and understand their actions in the garden to be the only reason for the Incarnation. One way or another, the Christian teachings around original, personal and 'establishment/structural' sin will always play a central part in any theology that seeks to probe ever more deeply into the mystery of the relationship between God and humanity. It is clear that most practising Catholics cannot conceive of any reason for the Word-become-flesh other than that of the fate-filled happenings involving two perfect people, a talking snake and an apple. This is so because most of us have been brought up with such a notion. That is why almost all our self-awareness, as Church, has to do with redemption and salvation. The drift and thrust of most of our cautions from the Vatican, of our weekly homilies and of our sacramental catechesis, for instance, is almost totally centred on strategies for encountering, coping with or escaping from, a strange and threatening world. Many a new day will dawn before the hoped-for paradigm shift outlined in these pages will once again become the traditional norm for Catholic doctrine, liturgy and life.

From the earliest Christian times the issue of original sin, personal sin and the sin of the world has been hotly debated whenever a theology of creation, of nature and grace, is proclaimed. Since St Augustine's initial definition of our traditional understanding of original sin, its physical transmission, the necessity of infant baptism, and the centrality of 'the Fall', many more wise and holy women and men have tried to offer a more loving, hopeful and positive picture of creation, incarnation and the light and darkness of humanity. Julian of Norwich wrote that: 'First there was the fall. Then there was salvation. And they were both the mercy of God.' In *Redemptor Hominis* (1979), Pope John Paul II's first 'Encyclical Letter to the Church', he does not dwell on this doctrine. He includes it, of course, but does not make it the sole cause of the Incarnation. Karl Rahner, too, maintains that the fall of humanity was not the first and only reason for revelation and salvation. He reminds us of the Scotist school of thought which holds that the most basic motive for revelation was not 'the blotting out of sin', but that the Incarnation was already the goal of the divine plan even apart from any divine foreknowledge of freely incurred guilt and sin.

There is no need here to go into the history of a long debate which surfaced on many occasions throughout the centuries, beginning within the lifetime of Jesus, then with Irenaeus, Duns Scotus, the mystics, Thomas Aquinas, St Francis, Teilhard de Chardin, M. D. Chenu, Edward Schillebeeckx, Rosemary Ruether, Roland Murphy, Sally McFague and many, many others. These writers open up new horizons to us. But the required shift in our consciousness and awareness will never come easy. Even though our hearts, being fashioned in the divine image, are already coded for such good news, what is carved into the psyche for centuries will not be reshaped in a day. And even when the rethinking begins, there will be many doubts. We need to study, to reflect on and work together on these profound theological issues concerning free-will, evil and salvation.

A renewed and more enlightened understanding of the meaning of incarnation is of vital importance to our questions about the role of the church in the world. Once it is clarified that we are not merely a 'fallen race in a fallen world', that Jesus Christ came not just to atone for our sins of complicity in the Garden, that the sacraments are infinitely more than a protection from our own relentless tendencies towards evil, then everything changes. The church can be seen to exist so that our inherent sacredness can be recognised and affirmed; so that the image of God can be brought to perfection within us; so that the divinisation of our humanity can be achieved. The *Dogmatic Constitution on Revelation* supports this theological stance when it sees Christ as both the salvation *and* completion of God's first loving desire.[57]

Original or personal?

In none of the Hebrew or Christian scriptures can you find a clear-cut distinction between personal and original sin. There is no perfectly innocent human being because, living in an unavoidable situation of sin and fragmentation, all of us become personally entangled in it. Theologian Monika Hellwig, holds that sin is a break with the right order and harmony of God's world which sets things awry in it and complicates life for everybody. To strike another is to arouse anger and evoke a whole chain of violent acts. To be unfaithful in one marriage is to cause a faint, diffuse anxiety in all marriages. To cheat or defraud or betray a secret, even once, is to start ripples of fear and distrust through the whole society. There is a world of sin around. It is into this world that each baby is born. St Paul speaks, not of original sin but of 'the sin of the world'. Baptism prepares us for the encounter with this sinful state.

It is not the arbitrary edict of God that people should pay the penalty for the supposed sin of those who went before them. Nor is the transmission of the sin in the act of procreation itself. It is because of the way we are constituted that our lives are so largely shaped by those who have lived before us. As individuals we are not made out of nothing but out of history. No one really starts with a clean slate.

The idea that 'baptism forgives original sin' is unknown to the church of the first few centuries. St Paul presupposes that the gift of God's life precedes the mystery of evil, even apart from baptism. The term 'original sin', as we saw, arose with St Augustine and his defence of infant baptism. Scripture does not suggest that the 'sin of the world' is passed to each person by generation. It seems to suggest, rather, that it is passed on by society, culture, upbringing and the experience of human relationships. Seeing the corporate personality of original sin, the writer Tresmontant has suggested that it is not so much the race inheriting the sin of an individual as the individual inheriting the sin of the race.

There is general agreement among our leading scripture scholars that the story of Adam's sin is a message about humanity as we know it, not about the beginning of humanity. It concerns the way that people stand before God all the time, not a historical description of how the first man and woman fell before God. It is only now that the damaging confusion of myth and history regarding the Adamic narratives is being addressed.

Theologians seem to be in agreement that the central emphasis on original sin has grown out of all proportion in the Christian scheme of things, negatively affecting and distorting the church's understanding of its role and mission in the world. Juan Segundo draws our attention to the two kinds of theology that attempt to explain some of the key 'moments' in salvation-history. There is a false and deadly step taken by a theology that attempts to link too closely the fact of creation with Eden, the fact of a 'fall' with a couple called Adam and Eve, and the beginning of salvation with what happened two thousand years ago.

On the other hand, a renewed, incarnational theology looks for the meaning of original sin in terms of the fact that people sin and become corrupt; the sin of Adam is in our own selves. It lies in the desperate struggle of the species and the person for survival, but also in the deliberate and egotistical choice for supremacy, for control, for possessions, for prestige, for revenge, for punishment. It is a 'going astray', a recklessness, a madness, a sickness, as Scripture puts it. Something goes wrong in us, an imbalance sets in, a good drive grows 'out of true'.

Saving my soul?
Leonard Cohen's song 'Anthem' states in the refrain 'There is a crack in everything. That's how the light gets in.' We do carry our treasure in earthen vessels. Richard Rohr OFM suggests that these are poetic ways of naming what we unfortunately call *original sin* – 'a poor choice of words', he says, 'because the word "sin" implies fault and culpability, and that is precisely not the point!' In one of his Daily Meditations Fr Rohr writes, 'Original sin was trying to warn us that there is a flaw at the heart of reality, that there is "a crack in everything", and so we should not be surprised when it shows itself in us or in everything else. This has the power to keep us patient, humble and less judgemental … The work of religion is to make you aware that something is already happening and you are a part of it. What we call "sins" are simply obstacles to that knowing, experiencing, participating.'

Resistance, tension, friction and concupiscence in themselves are neutral, necessary and given. But out of alignment, the great human spirit runs amok in confusion, destruction and, eventually, terrible evil. 'These forces of resistance and concupiscence,' writes Segundo in his *Evolution and Guilt*, 'in their specific meanings and contexts intended here, are not erased by baptism but rather given the communitarian possibility for opting for synthesis.'[58] While redemption ended the 'enslavement to sin', it gives us a greater responsibility for our decisions. Baptism, then, is seen as the sacrament of community, and of personal growth within it. It is not all about 'saving my own soul'. We save our souls by saving others. Cardinal Hume took this line of approach in one of his Reflections: 'In the past Catholics have been accused, perhaps with some justice, of stressing personal sinfulness and guilt and of over-emphasising the need for individual salvation. Today, we need to proclaim not only these, but also the fact that an individual is made for communion and community. We are also called to save the world and witness to the kingdom. There is no 'secular' realm from which God is absent. His presence in the world may be hidden and even denied, but God is everywhere. Therefore we must seek God in all the experiences of life and in all that is … The truth is that the Church has not a purely spiritual character but is intimately involved in the building of the kingdom in the human city. The new heaven and the new earth are not only to be longed for in the next life, but are to be established here and now.'

What is significant about these words of the Cardinal is the fact that he is interpreting the phenomenon of original sin, not in narrow historical and individualistic terms, but in the wider terms of a world in dire need of wholeness and healing, of the need for completion and fulfilment. He sees the mystery of incarnation as not just about the later putting right of something that went horribly wrong at the beginning, not just the desperate saving of an almost lost cause through the sin of our mythical ancestors, but also about the vindication of the first creation, the affirmation of God's presence in everything that is, the delight of God in what God has made, whether or not there was some kind of historical 'fall'.

In this instance, the role of the church is about the emphasis on original joy and blessing as well as, or rather than, on original sin and guilt; on affirming the glory of creation rather than on continually cautioning about its ambiguity and falsity; on pointing out the love and meaning to be discovered in daily life rather than on creating a dualistic dichotomy between the natural and the supernatural. The Church exists, in part, to clarify the fact that if there is any line to be drawn, it is not the boundary-line between Church and world, between 'good' people and 'bad' people, between life and death, between angels and devils. What is clarified is that if such a line is drawn (if we agree to use such unsubtle terminology), it is drawn between authentic and inauthentic living, between sheer greed and a magnanimous attitude, between the truly human and the falsely human, between trusting and suspicion, between hoping and being cynical, between forgiveness and revenge.

Sin is blind to beauty

In light of the preceding pages some other descriptions of sin come to mind. In Alice Walker's *The Colour Purple* the character Shug reminds us how fed-up God must be when we walk through a field of poppies and fail to notice the colour purple. Rabbi Lionel Blue refers to an admonition in *The Talmud*. On the final Judgement Day we shall be called to account for all the beautiful things we should have enjoyed – and didn't. Patrick Kavanagh, one of Ireland's finest poets, explains why a parish priest is worried about the spirituality of his new curate. The younger man was never full of wonder or reverence when the sun opened a flower. Sin is blind to beauty. It is grey and has no imagination. Sin shrinks before surprise and excitement. It sees no magic in creation. The vibrant presence of the Holy Spirit in all things is denied. Cynicism replaces trust. Sin lives in a flat world and fears the edges. Like a depressed soul, it does not notice colour.

Sin is more than lots of sins. It is not a 'one-off' mistake in an otherwise perfect life, a clearly-defined stain on a white surface. It is more like a way of being that we follow, an attitude of refusal to the invitation to wholeness and holiness. Sin is a draining thing. It has no growing in it. It is ugly because it is graceless. It cannot bless or rejoice or be passionate. Nor does it want to see very far. Shades of this negative state are alive and well in all of us. To believe anything else would be mad beyond measure.

Sin is the choice to live in illusion, to avoid the truth of existence, of light, of one's dark side. Many people experience sin as being trapped, tempted to despair, being held captive. Others speak of sin in terms of fear, fear of self, of others, of taking risks, of speaking out. Such sin is the refusal to trust that God is good and that therefore we are good too. This results in a life of excessive control, of clinging to the ego-self, of grasping for more, of trying to prove that we are worthy because we cannot trust in unconditional love. Sin is giving in to self-hate and to the insecurity that results in a life focused on self-protection at the expense of others.

When I think of sin I think of fear – the fear of beauty, of pleasure, of change and of being open. Closed-ness must be *the* sin against the Holy Spirit. Deep-seated insecurity keeps the shutters tight.

There is no light where there is no trust. Many of us were brought up in a climate of fear where to be different was to be avoided. We lived in a two-tiered world where only the top tier mattered. Lie low here and fly high in heaven. Steer clear of all risk in this life so as to enjoy the no-risk existence to follow. There is something sinful about this blind attitude towards the divine invitation to live life to the full, in the here and now. In scriptural terms sin is seen as 'missing the mark'. It misses the miracle. There is no mystery in the life of sin. In his famous *Original Blessing*, Matthew Fox writes, 'By sinning in this way we refuse to fall in love with life, to love what is loveable, to befriend and savour life's simple and non-elitist pleasures, to celebrate the blessings of life, to return thanks for such blessings by still more blessing.'[59]

For centuries, there has been a major element in our Roman Catholic belief system that sees the Church as in conflict with the world, as a beacon of truth in a tunnel of lies, as a recipe for life in a culture of death, as a ship of saints in a sea of fools. But grace, as we have seen, is not like that. This book is dedicated to renewing the original meaning and vision of grace for all God's people, for the victimised and abused parts of all of us, because it makes a heaven or a hell of a difference whether the church in which we find ourselves points to humanity as a sin to be atoned for, or a blessing to be celebrated.

One Ordinary Table of Mystery

What is truly personal is truly universal

What is so delightful and profound about the Mass, the summit and source of our Christian lives, is its unfathomable mystery. It can be explored in terms of its sacrificial-meal dimensions, its aspects of praise and thanksgiving, its themes of covenant and conversion. I wish now only to reflect on its significance as the sacrament of our daily lives: the sacrament which gives meaning and therefore healing to every single thought, feeling and action from dawn to dusk and from dusk to dawn: the sacrament of our astounding universe whose long-held secrets are only now being revealed through the miracles of scientific discovery.

When conversation touches hearts, the mystery is engaged and aspects of Eucharistic living emerge. Every shared sandwich or brilliant banquet is a moment of grace if people stop playing games and sensitively encounter each other in the search for truth. Sometimes the exchanges will be heavy and serious, sometimes playful and humorous. Either way they are the raw material of Eucharistic celebration. What is meant by this?

Think of the levels of emotion within the experiences of people as they care for their happy and sick babies, as they try to cope with success and failure bringing shared joy or depression, as they are overwhelmed by the agony and ecstasy of their relationships in conflict and reconciliation, as they commit themselves to a project or long-held desire for equality or justice, for a new age of peace. Such passion and commitment are of the essence of our lives as parents, family, friends, lovers, colleagues, neighbours, responsible citizens and, I'm afraid, as perennial sinners. Finally, multiply such moments *ad infinitum* all over the universe both now and during its long history.

Now think of the God who lives in the profoundest depths of all of us. And think, because of God's incarnation in each human spirit from the first creation – an intimacy only fully revealed later on at the first Christmas – of the possibility that maybe every human emotion and its expression in word or glance or touch, is at the heart of God's emergence within the human community: that this is the divine intimacy of continuing incarnation, the evolving warp and weft of the fabric of God's design for our contemporary society. Is it possible to believe that all of this is celebrated as often as we go to Mass?

The table of the Eucharist stretches wider still. Our Catholic tradition protects a deep Christian cosmology enshrined in the elemental symbols of bread and wine. Current literature is beginning to resurrect a most moving and beautiful sacramental theology where the Eucharistic liturgy assumes cosmic significance. This is the aspect of our weekend worship that theologian Fr Dermot Lane hopes will be more imaginatively celebrated, especially today, 'in view of the presence of so much ecological degradation and destruction of God's creation'.[60]

Every time we celebrate the saving mystery, we remember and reactivate God's initial creative work and God's subsequent and continuing redemptive action in the past and present. We affirm, celebrate and intensify the constant presence of grace in our midst from the fiery beginning of our cosmic story, through the billions of years of evolution, into the current thrusting, straining and groaning of the world, forever painfully giving birth to new beauty. In the *Prologue* to his Gospel, John reminds us that Love has always been incarnate. That is the mighty love story that we celebrate around the table of the Lord of the Universe. The celebration is about the liberating force of this sacred memory, with its assurance about the wholeness and holiness of all the dimensions of creation.

It is prophetic in signalling a most powerful counter-sign to the dualistic and divisive greed that is decimating the resources of mother earth.

Getting our minds, or rather our imaginations, around all of this is not easy. That is why we are gifted with the Eucharist. The Eucharist is the sacrament of the holiness of these loving and community-building aspirations that are forever birthed in the human heart. It is the weekly reminder and guarantee that this is so, that nothing is wasted, that all in the end is harvest. The widespread and deep-seated mistake of dualism, whereby, as we have seen (p. 139), the sacred is set up as over against the secular, makes it very difficult for many searching Christians to feel secure in such a neglected but thoroughly orthodox tradition. While their hearts rejoice in the recognition of this beautiful vision of the love and meaning at the centre of life, their minds are conditioned by a grimmer and more barren story of a basically wicked world.

The amazing insight we grapple with today is about the humanity of God, the focus of the real presence of Jesus in our world, the intimate movement of the indwelling Spirit within our most secret and often ambiguous desires. A creation spirituality is dedicated to identifying the authentic presence of God in the emerging experiences of everyone. Whether trivial or important, whether about disappointments or achievements, whether about fear, hope or pain – in these places we find what spiritual writer Hugh Lavery called 'the really real'.

The astonishing revelation of Incarnation

What I'm trying to clarify and identify here, is the locus or address of the truest reality of the human spirit. Having explored that, I'm then trying to emphasise that here, too, is the holiest and most authentic experience of the divine. A fully-fleshed and full-blooded theology of incarnation, unique among all other religious traditions of revelation, contains the almost incredible truth that here, and here only, and for us humans, is the only way of experiencing God. It is becoming more obvious from recent theological writings about the original Christian vision of incarnation, together with a trust in the teachings about 'developing doctrine', that a whole forgotten model of traditional sacramental theology is waiting to be rediscovered and explored.

Karl Rahner reminds us again and again that there is no event in which we cannot experience God. There is nothing in life so secular or sinful that we cannot find God in it. It means that we live in a very ambiguous world, which is, in fact, permeated by grace. The Eucharist is not a refuge from a trivial or commonplace world. We should never treat it as an escape from the emptiness and meaninglessness of our lives. God is in the most commonplace events, happenings and experiences of each day, even the ones that seem furthest from heaven. To believe this is an immense challenge. Why would God want to be present to such 'ordinary' moments? But if we have the courage and patience to look, we may be surprised to find a God more beautiful and loving than we dared to dream of.

According to Rahner, each moment of our lives is like a grain of sand lying just alongside the ocean of mystery. Every event, no matter how profane or mundane it might seem, is a potential experience of God. In fact, the experience of God does not normally take place in religious ways and at sacred times, but in the material of the failures, difficulties, responsibility, fidelity, forgiveness of the human condition. Michael Skelley in *The Liturgy of the World: Karl Rahner's Theology of Worship* writes, 'The explicitly religious moments of our lives, experiences of the church's liturgy, for example, are necessary and important symbolic manifestations of the presence of God in all our moments. But they are just that; they are not the only times that God is present. We will only be able to recognise the presence of the absolute mystery in the liturgy if we first recognise its abiding presence throughout our whole lives and in all the world.'[61]

After the resurrection, in the powerful experience of fellowship and community, the disciples indeed realised that Jesus, surrounded by sinners and outcasts, had given to the breaking of bread a new and universal meaning – not just in terms of the Passover meal, but in relation to all meals and encounters between people, from the innocent child's shared midday apple to the executive's more ambiguous banquet, wherever in fact reconciliation and trust and hope for the future are happening. Since the paschal mystery is really present in every attempt to relate and reconcile what is broken, to recover and discover the energy of love, to create and to grow in trust, then the human predicament itself is the central dynamism for the specifically ecclesial celebration of Eucharist.

Conscious of what has been achieved and revealed in Christ's death and resurrection, the Church carries the table of the world to the table of the Eucharist for its interpretation, purification, transformation and completion. It can do no less, 'for the partaking of the Body and Blood of Christ does nothing other than transform us into that which we consume'.[62] The pattern of a true and loving humanity revealed in Jesus, is the only paradigm for our actions and attitudes. Because Jesus lived a human life, thought with a human mind, loved with a human heart and was tempted in his human condition, nothing, apart from deliberate, persistent and unrepentant destruction of love, is other than the raw material of the Eucharist.[63]

Theologian Tissa Balasuriya in *The Eucharist and Human Liberation*, quotes from Tagore's *The Hidden God*:

> *Leave this singing and chanting and telling of beads.*
> *Whom do you worship in this lonely dark corner of the temple with all the doors shut?*
> *Open your eyes and see that God is not in front of you.*
> *He is there where the farmer is tilling the hard ground and where the labourer is breaking stones.*
> *He is with them in the sun and the rain and his garment is covered with dust.*
> *Put off your holy cloak and, like him, come down on to the dusty soil.*
> *Our master himself has joyfully taken on the bonds of creation; he is bound with us forever.*
> *Come out of your private devotions and leave aside the incense.*
> *What harm is there if your clothes become tattered and stained?*
> *Meet him and stand by him in the toil and in the sweat of your brow.*[64]

In his Jubilee letter, *Tertio Millennio Adveniente*, Pope John Paul II, calling for 'a new springtime of Christianity', had intimations of the cosmic nuances of preparing for the third millennium. He was well aware of the significance of creation theology in this regard. 'The fact that in the fullness of time the Eternal Word took on the condition of a creature, gives a unique cosmic value to the event which took place in Bethlehem two thousand years ago. Thanks to the Word, the world of creatures appears as a cosmos, an ordered universe. And it is the same Word who, by taking flesh, renews the cosmic order of creation.'

Creation had waited for billions of years to achieve self-consciousness. Once this breakthrough was accomplished, the cosmos then needed to celebrate its incredible life-story with its mysterious beginning, its hazardous evolution, its split-second timing and its relentless success. For with the advent of humanity – its new and unique heart and mind – this became possible. After the Incarnation, the Eucharist is one of its richest celebratory expressions. And this expression has to be symbolic – encapsulated in time and space. 'The earth, like an apple, is placed on the table.' Around the table bearing the fruits of the earth and the work of human hands, through the human voices, gestures and sacramental ceremonial of its offspring, the very cosmos itself is in worship before its God, offering itself to its incomprehensible lover-God in the ecstasy of its joys and the bitterness of its sorrows.

Cosmic Intimacy – Incarnation and Eucharist
Just as we filtered the passion and glory of human living and loving through the lens of the Passover of Jesus as celebrated in the Eucharist, thus revealing the presence of the living God incarnate, so too with the glories of the galaxies. The play and struggle between the dying and rising in the loving heart of the living cosmos, together with the eventual outcome of delight of a sometimes bloody conflict, is revealed, clarified, named, owned and celebrated by the universe at every true Eucharistic gathering, 'with a directness and an intensity like that of the incarnation itself', as John Macquarrie puts it in his *Principles of Christian Theology*.[65] Thus

in a ritual in time and space, involving bread and wine and words, in one privileged and symbolic moment, the eternal significance of the mighty cosmos is carefully embraced and forever celebrated. In his prose-poem *Hymn of the Universe*, de Chardin moves our hearts: 'I will place on my paten, O God, the harvest to be won, this morning, by the renewal of daily labour. Into my chalice I shall pour all the sap which is to be pressed out this day from the fruits of the earth ... All the things of the world to which this day will bring increase; all those that will diminish; all those that will die ... This is the material of my sacrifice ... The offering you really want, the offering you mysteriously need every day to appease your hunger, to slake your thirst, is nothing less than the growth of the world borne ever onwards in the stream of universal becoming.'[66]

In the dynamic presence of the bread and wine on the table, we have symbolised just about everything that can be predicated of humanity, of the earth and everything in it and on it – its flora and fauna, of the universe and the cosmos itself – the past, the present and the future of all creation. All labour is therefore holy. All true work, as the Prophet tells us, is love made visible. These rich and simple elements gather up the intense flow and counter-flow of the world, its darkness and light, its failures and mistakes, its strivings and hopes, its indomitable creativity. Theologian Fr Dermot Lane writes that 'By previewing the future, the Eucharist gives a focus, a sense of direction, to a world that is in danger of losing sight of gifted origins and graced endings.'

And then the eternal words of divine disclosure and universal revelation are spoken: *This is my Body*. They sound around the earth like the angels' Christmas song and the *tenebrae* of Good Friday. They echo off the stars with the energy of transfiguration. They were first whispered by our Creator-Parent as the terrible beauty of the fiery atoms shattered the infinite darkness of nothingness with unimaginable flame, heat and light. And they are whispered again, a thousand times a day, in the midst of God's holy people around a table with a piece of bread and a cup of wine. *This is my Body*. It is God-become-atom, become-galaxies, become-universes, become-Earth, become-flesh, become-everything. It is a kind of *Angelus* of hope – a remembering, a reminding, a recapitulation and a confirming that the divine and the human, the sacred and the secular, the holy and the profane, are all God's one body by virtue of creation, first in time but revealed to us later, and once for all, in the ultimate gift of meaning, the Incarnation.

But there is a death at the heart of all growing and liberating. The seed must die. As we take, break, share, eat and drink the cosmic bread and wine and turn to embrace the stranger at the 'kiss of peace', how aware are we of the kind of dying we may be called upon to make? And we must believe that our efforts will bear fruit even though we may never live to see that harvest.

In *Tomorrow's Child* Rubem Alves writes, 'Let us plant dates, even though those who plant them will never eat them … We must live by the love of what we will never see. This is the secret discipline. It is a refusal to let the creative act be dissolved away in immediate sense experience, and a stubborn commitment to the future of our grandchildren. Such disciplined love is what has given prophets, revolutionaries and saints the courage to die for the future they envisaged. They make their own bodies the seed of their highest hopes.'[67]

In one sense we are at the beginning now. There is a mission of cosmic proportions to be accomplished – a world to win and a universe to save, God's body to be healed. A massive re-education of mind and heart is called for. There is, it seems to me, a readiness for change, a potential for transformation. There is a growing sensitivity to new strategies of concern, a kind of genetic awareness of the need for imminent action. There are pockets of conspirators all over the world; and when these small streams of consciousness seem to make but little headway into the dry mainland, we must believe that at another invisible level, the waves of transformation are already sweeping through. In his 'Say not, the struggle nought availeth' poet Arthur Hugh Clough wrote:

> *For while the tired waves, vainly breaking,*
> *Seem here no painful inch to gain,*
> *Far back, through creeks and inlets making,*
> *Comes silent, flooding in, the main.*[68]

Creation made Flesh

In recent discussions, liturgists and believing scientists have been considering how the intrinsic connection between the Mass and the evolving world itself can be explored and expressed in our worship. Put another way, how can the Mass be understood as a cosmic moment? Will this touch something deep in all of us and transform our hearts?

For a start, a truly incarnational theology of liturgy insists that our ritual acts of worship must never be seen as isolated interventions of grace into our 'merely' secular lives and world. Rather are they the symbolic expressions of the holiness of Creation itself. This is hugely significant and takes some explaining.

The Incarnation of God did not only happen in Bethlehem two thousand years ago. The first incarnation actually began with a moment we now call the 'Big Bang' or the 'silent flaring forth'. Two thousand years ago, the human Incarnation of God in Jesus happened, but before that, in the original incarnation of the amazing story of evolution, God had already begun the mysterious process of becoming flesh by first becoming Creation itself.

St Bonaventure and Blessed John Duns Scotus held that the whole of Creation was the necessary preparation for the divine Incarnation in Jesus, the Human One. The fleshing of God was not a later rescue attempt to put the original, failed plan back on track. Fall or no fall, it was lovingly willed from the very beginning.

'Creation', wrote St Thomas Aquinas, 'is the primary and most perfect revelation of the Divine … If we do not understand Creation correctly, we cannot hope to understand God correctly.' Neither will we grasp the quintessence of eucharistic celebration. 'The only real fall of man', wrote Alexander Schmemann, 'is his non eucharistic life in a non eucharistic world.'[69]

The story can be told like this. An eternally self-giving Parent-God, already incarnate in Creation, had waited for billions of years to achieve self-consciousness in the human heart and mind. In the words of Julian Huxley, quoted by Pierre Teilhard de Chardin, 'humanity discovers that it is nothing else than evolution become conscious of itself'. And, at the appointed time, after this long infancy, the Human One was born.

Moving beyond the destructive doctrines of atonement-centred theologies, cosmologist and cultural historian Thomas Berry points out that Jesus did not come into the world, added on later, so to speak, as a necessary afterthought; he came into a world that was made originally in and through himself as the creative context of all existence.

Against this horizon, we are invited to understand the Mass as the sacramental moment of an astonishing revelation – the revelation of the love and meaning hidden in the first moment of Creation; the revelation of the burning presence of God warming and preparing the earth as a cradle of welcome for Christ; the revelation that the history of evolution is the genealogy of the Baby. In receiving Holy Communion, we experience the soul of the earth.

The Eucharist encapsulates forever this enduring song of love at the core of the cosmos. In the sacramental mode, Fr Berry holds, with bread and wine, the world is acknowledging and celebrating its very being as flowing from the womb of God at the beginning of time, and in each passing moment moving inevitably towards its divine fulfilment in Christ. He identifies the Christ story with the story of the universe.

The Eucharist carries sublime significance when understood as the deepest symbol of the hidden secrets already buried and burning in the core of Creation. It is the liturgical expression of the living river of love that streamed out at the beginning of time and now flows everywhere.

That love sustains the cosmos of our hearts and the heart of our cosmos, 'groaning in [their] one great act of giving birth', in their long journey home. That is why the physical world itself is the incarnate body of God and will enjoy the same future as we will. The mighty mystery of graced, universal evolution is encapsulated in one ordinary, daily sacramental moment. Every Mass is a cosmic event!

'Yes, cosmic!' John Paul II exclaims in *Ecclesia de Eucharistia*. 'Because even when the Eucharist is celebrated on the humble altar of a country church, it is always, in some way, celebrated on the altar of the world. It unites heaven and earth. It embraces, permeates and celebrates all Creation.'[70] In his *Feast of Faith*, he explains why 'Christian liturgy must be cosmic liturgy, why it must, as it were, orchestrate the mystery of Christ with all the voices of Creation.'

In his poetic, eucharistic reflections, especially in his *Le Milieu Divin*, priest-scientist de Chardin sees the sacramental species as formed by the totality of the world. And he perceives the duration of Creation, 'the growth of the world borne ever onwards', as the time needed for its consecration.

The unfolding of the secrets of the phenomenon called life, in all its personal, earthly and cosmic dimensions, with its fearful darkness and irresistible brightness, is the bread and wine of God's universal becoming. Without the Eucharist we would surely forget that our beautiful God is very incarnate indeed!

Endnotes

Part One

1 Kavanagh, *Collected Poems*, 2005. p. 72.
2 In Mitchell, ed., *The Enlightened Heart*, 1993. pp. 38–9.
3 Thomas, *Selected Poems*, 1996.
4 Auden, *Collected Poems*, 2007. p. 530.
5 Cassidy, *Good Friday People*, 1991.
6 'God's Grandeur' in Hopkins, *The Major Works of Gerard Manley Hopkins*, 1986.
7 Teilhard de Chardin, *The Divine Milieu*, 2004. pp. 20–3.
8 Moriarty, *Nostos*, 2001.
9 Copus, *The Shuttered Eye*, 1996.
10 Irion, *Yes, World*, 1970.
11 Motion, *Selected Poems*, 2002.
12 From 'Four Interrupted Prayers' in Barks, *The Soul of Rumi*, 2001.
13 'A Christmas Childhood' in Kavanagh, *Collected Poems*, 2005. p. 40.
14 'A Christmas Childhood' in Kavanagh, *Collected Poems*, 2005. p. 40.
15 'A Christmas Childhood' in Kavanagh, *Collected Poems*, 2005. p. 40.
16 *The Great Hunger* in Kavanagh, *Collected Poems*, 2005. p. 72.
17 'The One' in Kavanagh, *Collected Poems*, 2005. p. 229.
18 'A Christmas Childhood' in Kavanagh, *Collected Poems*, 2005. p. 40.
19 'Advent' in Kavanagh, *Collected Poems*, 2005. p. 111.
20 Hesketh, *The Leave Train*, 1994.
21 Baldovin, *Reforming the Liturgy*, 2009.
22 Dickinson, *The Poems of Emily Dickinson*, 2005.
23 Oliver, *Dream Work*, 1986. p. 62.
24 Oliver, *Why I Wake Early*, 2004. pp. 34–5.
25 Okri, *Birds of Heaven*, 1995.
26 Roberts, *Corpus*, 2004.
27 Roberts, *Rosa Mundi*, 2011.
28 In Mitchell, ed., *The Enlightened Heart*, 1993. pp. 38–9.
29 In Christian, *Philosophy*, 2012.
30 Oliver, *Swan*, 2010.

31 Cassidy, *Good Friday People*, 1991.
32 Lewis, *Mere Christianity*, 2001.
33 Thomas, *Collected Later Poems 1988–2000*, 2004. p. 131.
34 de Saint Exupéry, *Wind, Sand and Stars*, 1939.
34 Clare of Assisi, *The Lady*, 2006. p. 57.
36 Williams, *True Resurrection*, 1983.
37 Straub, 'Mud Pies & Kites', *Gerry Straub's Blog*, 2011.
38 O'Connor in *Africa*, 2011.
39 Coxhead, 'Keeping Silence', *Desert Call*, 2012.
40 'Shaper Shaped' in Gokak, ed., *The Golden Treasury of Indo–Anglian Poetry*, 1970. p. 198.
41 Smith, *Great Moments of Sportsmanship & Extraordinary Sports People*, 2008.
42 Whyte, *Where Many Rivers Meet*, 1990.
43 Ashbery, *A Wave*, 1985. p. 1.
44 Sarton, *Collected Poems*, 1993.
45 Dostoevsky, *The Idiot*, 1996. p. 356.
46 Macmurray, *Freedom in the Modern World*, 1996.
47 Thomas, *The Minister*, 1953.
48 Harries, *Art and the Beauty of God*, 1993.
49 O'Connell, *One Clear Call*, 2003.
50 Woodruff, *Meditations with Mechtild of Magdeburg*, 1982.
51 Masefield, *Spunyarn*, 2011. p. 6.
52 Whyte, *The House of Belonging*, 1997.
53 In Paul, *The Complete Poems of Rabindranath Tagore's* Gitanjali, 2006. p. 169.
54 Brueggemann, *Finally Comes the Poet*, 1989.
55 Brueggemann, *Finally Comes the Poet*, 1989.

Part Two

1 'The Liturgy of the Hours according to the Roman Rite', *The Office of Readings*. Vol. III, p. 510.
2 'God's Grandeur' in Hopkins, *The Major Works of Gerard Manley Hopkins*, 1986.
3 Joseph Mary Plunkett quoted in Bausch, *Once Upon a Gospel*, 2008. p. 163.
4 'God's Grandeur' in Hopkins, *The Major Works of Gerard Manley Hopkins*, 1986.
5 John Paul II, *Letter to Artists*, 1999.
6 Teilhard de Chardin, *The Divine Milieu*, 2004. p. 17.
7 In Benner, *Contemplative Vision*, 2011. p. 162.

8   Skelley, *The Liturgy of the World*, 1991. p. 100.
9   Rahner, 'Secular Life and the Sacraments: 1: A Copernican Revolution', *The Tablet*, 1971. p. 237.
10 Benedict, *Saint Benedict's Rule*, 2004. Ch. 31, p. 97.
11 Rahner, *Theological Investigations*, 1973. Vol. xiv, p. 166.
12 Fagan, 'Sacraments and the Spiritual Life', *Doctrine and Life*, 1973. p. 40.
13 Fagan, 'Sacraments and the Spiritual Life', *Doctrine and Life*, 1973. p. 42.
14 Macquarrie, *Principles of Christian Theology*, 1966.
15 Skelley, *The Liturgy of the World*, 1991. p. 71.
16 Fox, *Sheer Joy*, 1992.
17 Fox, *Sheer Joy*, 1992.
18 Fox, *Sheer Joy*, 1992.
19 Eucharistic Prayer III – old translation.
20 Christmas Preface III – old translation.
21 Wilder, *The Ides of March*, 1964 quoted in Fransen, *Divine Grace and Man*, 1965.
22 Fransen, *Divine Grace and Man*, 1965. p. 173.
23 Mackey, 'Theology 20: Grace', *The Furrow*, 1973. p. 341.
24 Kiesling, 'Paradigms of Sacramentality', *Worship*, 1970. p. 426.
25 Baum, *Man Becoming*, 1971. pp. 75–6.
26 Sölle, *Thinking about God*, 1990.
27 Rahner, 'The Mass and the World: Secular Life and the Sacraments: 2', *The Tablet*, 1971. p. 267.
28 Kiesling, 'Paradigms of Sacramentality', *Worship*, 1970.
29 Kiesling, 'Paradigms of Sacramentality', *Worship*, 1970. p. 426.
30 *Gaudium et Spes*, par. 22.
31 Ladinsky, *I Heard God Laughing*, 1996. p. 85.
32 Skelley, *The Liturgy of the World*, 1991.
33 Rahner, *The Eternal Year*, 1991. p. 91.
34 King, *Pierre Teilhard de Chardin*, 1999. p. 14.
35 King, *Pierre Teilhard de Chardin*, 1999. p. 42.
36 Johnson, *Quest for the Living God*, 2011. p. 181.
37 O'Murchu, *In the Beginning was the Spirit*, 2012. p. 206.
38 O'Murchu, *In the Beginning was the Spirit*, 2012.
39 O'Murchu, *In the Beginning was the Spirit*, 2012.
40 Teilhard de Chardin, *Hymn of the Universe*, 1966. p. 76.
41 Cannato, *Field of Compassion*, 2010.
42 Berry, *The Dream of the Earth*, 1990.
43 Berry, *The Dream of the Earth*, 1990. p. 106.
44 Swimme explains: 'I say four million years because though it's difficult to identify where we should mark the beginning of humanity, one way to proceed is to take the origin as that moment when our ancestors first began walking on two legs.' Swimme, *The Hidden Heart of the Cosmos*, 1996. pp. 1–2.

45 Swimme, *The Hidden Heart of the Cosmos*, 1996. p. 41.

46 Gorringe, *Earthly Visions*, 2011. p. 13.

47 Gorringe, *Earthly Visions*, 2011. p. 103.

48 Soskice, 'Art and Ideas: Painting and the Absence of Grace', *Modern Painters*, 1991.

49 Gorringe, *Earthly Visions*, 2011. p. 135.

50 Gorringe, *Earthly Visions*, 2011. p. 139.

51 Gorringe, *Earthly Visions*, 2011. p. 14.

52 Gorringe, *Earthly Visions*, 2011. p. 14.

53 Gorringe, *Earthly Visions*, 2011. pp. 192–3.

54 Lonergan and Maritain, *The Critical Spirit*, 2003. p. 207.

55 Maritain, *Education at the Crossroads*, 1943. p. 9.

56 Harries, *Art and the Beauty of God*, 1993. p. 113.

57 *Dei Verbum: Dogmatic Constitution on Divine Revelation*, par. 2, 3. See also *Gaudium et Spes*, par. 22.

58 Segundo, *Evolution and Guilt*, 1974. p. 51.

59 Fox, *Original Blessing*, 1983. p. 119.

60 Lane, *Christ at the Centre*, 1990. Ch. 6.

61 Skelley, *The Liturgy of the World*, 1991. p. 83.

62 *Lumen Gentium*, par. 26.

63 *Gaudium et Spes*, par. 22.

64 Balasuriya, *The Eucharist and Human Liberation*, 1979. p. 165.

65 Macquarrie, *Principles of Christian Theology*, 1966.

66 Teilhard de Chardin, *Hymn of the Universe*, 1966. pp. 19–20.

67 Alves, *Tomorrow's Child*, 1972. p. 76.

68 Clough, *Selected Poems*, 2003. p. 58.

69 Schmemann, *For the Life of the World*, 1973. p. 18.

70 John Paul II, *Ecclesia de Eucharistia*, 2003. par. 1.

Select Bibliography

ARTICLES, DOCUMENTS AND LETTERS

Benedict XVI, *Porta Fidei* (Vatican City, 2011).

Coxhead, Gillian, 'Keeping Silence', *Desert Call* (Winter 2012).

Fagan, Sean, 'Sacraments and the Spiritual Life', *Doctrine and Life*, 23/8 (1973).

John Paul II, *Ecclesia de Eucharistia* (Vatican City, 2003).

John Paul II, *Letter to Artists* (Vatican City, 1999).

Kiesling, Christopher, 'Paradigms of Sacramentality', *Worship*, 44/7 (1970), 422–32.

Mackey, James P., 'Theology 20: Grace', *The Furrow*, 24/6 (June 1973), pp. 338–52.

O'Connor, Tom, *Africa: St Patrick's Missions* (Dec. 2011).

Rahner, Karl, 'Secular Life and the Sacraments: 1: A Copernican Revolution', *The Tablet*, 225/6822 (6 Mar. 1971), pp. 236–8.

Rahner, Karl, 'The Mass and the World: Secular Life and the Sacraments: 2', *The Tablet*, 225/6823 (13 Mar. 1971), pp. 267–8.

Soskice, Oliver, 'Art and Ideas: Painting and the Absence of Grace', *Modern Painters*, 4/1 (Spring 1991), pp. 63–5.

Straub, Gerry, 'Mud Pies & Kites', *Gerry Straub's Blog* (Burbank, California, USA: Pax et Bonum Communications; pubd online May 2011) <http://gerrystraub. wordpress.com/2011/05/26/mud-pies-kites-2/> accessed 20 Feb. 2014.

Vatican Council II, *Dei Verbum: Dogmatic Constitution on Divine Revelation*, promulgated by Pope Paul VI (Vatican City, 1965).

Vatican Council II, *Gaudium et Spes: Pastoral Constitution on the Church in the Modern World*, promulgated by Pope Paul VI (Vatican City, 1965).

Vatican Council II, *Lumen Gentium: Dogmatic Constitution on the Church*, promulgated by Pope Paul VI (Vatican City, 1964).

BOOKS

Alves, Rubem A., *Tomorrow's Child: Imagination, Creativity and the Rebirth of Culture* (New York, New York, USA: Harper & Row, 1972).

Ashbery, John, *A Wave: Poems* (New York, New York, USA: Penguin Books, 1985).

Auden, W. H., *Collected Poems*, ed. Edward Mendelson (New York, New York, USA: Modern Library, 2007).

Balasuriya, Tissa, *The Eucharist and Human Liberation* (Maryknoll, New York, USA: Orbis Books, 1979).

Baldovin, John F., *Reforming the Liturgy: A Response to the Critics* (Collegeville, Minnesota, USA: Liturgical Press, 2009).

Barks, Coleman, *The Soul of Rumi: A New Collection of Ecstatic Poems* (New York, New York, USA: HarperCollins, 2001).

Baum, Gregory, *Man Becoming: God in Secular Experience* (New York, New York, USA: Herder and Herder, 1971).

Bausch, William J., *Once Upon a Gospel: Inspiring Homilies and Insightful Reflections* (New London, Connecticut, USA: Twenty-Third, 2008).

Benedict, *Saint Benedict's Rule*, tr. Patrick Barry (Mahwah, New Jersey, USA: HiddenSpring, 2004).

Benner, Juliet, *Contemplative Vision: A Guide to Christian Art and Prayer* (Downers Grove, Illinois, USA: InterVarsity Press, 2011).

Berry, Thomas, *The Dream of the Earth* (San Francisco, California, USA: Sierra Club Books, 1990).

Betjeman, John, *Collected Poems* (London, England: John Murray, 2006).

Bottrall, Ronald and Bottrall, Margaret, eds., *Collected English Verse* (London, England: Sidgwick & Jackson, 1969).

Brueggemann, Walter, *Finally Comes the Poet: Daring Speech for Proclamation* (Minneapolis, Minnesota, USA: Augsburg Fortress, 1989).

Cannato, Judy, *Field of Compassion: How the New Cosmology is Transforming Spiritual Life* (Notre Dame, Indiana, USA: Sorin Books, 2010).

Carr, Nicholas, *The Shallows: What the Internet is Doing to our Brains* (New York, New York, USA: W. W. Norton, 2010).

Cassidy, Sheila, *Good Friday People* (London, England: Darton, Longman & Todd, 1991).

Christian, James L., *Philosophy: An Introduction to the Art of Wondering* (Boston, Massachusetts, USA: Wadsworth Cengage Learning, 2012).

Clare of Assisi, *The Lady: Early Documents*, ed. Regis J. Armstrong (London, England: New City, 2006).

Clough, Arthur Hugh, *Selected Poems*, ed. Shirley Chew (New York, New York, USA: Routledge, 2003).

Congar, Yves, *My Journal of the Council*, tr. Mary John Ronayne, Mary Cecily Boulding and Denis Minns (Dublin, Ireland: Dominican, 2012).

Copus, Julia, *The Shuttered Eye* (Tarset, Northumberland, England: Bloodaxe Books, 1996).

de Saint Exupéry, Antoine, *Wind, Sand and Stars* (New York, New York, USA: Reynal & Hitchcock, 1939).

Dickinson, Emily, *The Poems of Emily Dickinson*, ed. R. W. Franklin (Cambridge, Massachusetts: Belknap Press, 2005).

Dostoevsky, Fyodor, *The Idiot* (Ware, Hertfordshire, England: Wordsworth Editions, 1996).

Fox, Matthew, *Original Blessing* (Santa Fe, New Mexico, USA: Bear, 1983).

Fox, Matthew, *Sheer Joy: Conversations with Thomas Aquinas on Creation Spirituality* (New York, New York, USA: HarperCollins, 1992).

Fransen, Peter, *Divine Grace and Man* (New York, New York, Mentor-Omega, 1965).

Gokak, Vinayak Krishna, ed., *The Golden Treasury of Indo–Anglian Poetry* (New Delhi, National Capital Territory of Delhi, India: Sahitya Akademi, 1970).

Gorringe, T. J., *Earthly Visions: Theology and the Challenges of Art* (London, England: Yale University Press, 2011).

Harries, Richard, *Art and the Beauty of God: A Christian Understanding* (London, England: Mowbray, 1993).

Hesketh, Phoebe, *The Leave Train: New and Selected Poems* (London, England: Enitharmon Press, 1994).

Hopkins, Gerard Manley, _The Major Works of Gerard Manley Hopkins_ (Oxford, Oxfordshire, England: Oxford World's Classics, 1986).

Irion, Mary Jean, _Yes, World: A Mosaic of Meditation_ (New York, New York, USA: R. W. Baron, 1970).

Johnson, Elizabeth A., _Quest for the Living God: Mapping Frontiers in the Theology of God_ (London, England: Continuum, 2011).

Kavanagh, Patrick, _Collected Poems_, ed. Antoinette Quinn (London, England: Penguin Books, 2005).

Kelly, Kevin T., _50 Years Receiving Vatican II: A Personal Odyssey_ (Dublin, Ireland: Columba Press, 2012).

Kelly, Tony, _An Expanding Theology: Faith in a World of Connections_ (Sydney, New South Wales, Australia: E. J. Dwyer, 1993).

King, Ursula, _Pierre Teilhard de Chardin_ (Maryknoll, New York, USA: Orbis Books, 1999).

Ladinsky, Daniel, _I Heard God Laughing: Renderings of Hafiz_ (Walnut Creek, California, USA: Sufism Reoriented, 1996).

Lane, Dermot A., _Christ at the Centre: Selected Issues in Christology_ (Dublin, Ireland: Veritas, 1990).

Lawrence, D. H., _The Complete Poems of D. H. Lawrence_ (Ware, Hertfordshire, England: Wordsworth Editions, 2002).

Lewis, C. S., _Mere Christianity_ (New York, New York, USA: HarperCollins, 2001).

Lonergan, Bernard and Maritain, Jacques, _The Critical Spirit_ (Dublin, Ireland: Columba Press, 2003).

Macmurray, John, _Freedom in the Modern World_ (Amherst, New York, USA: Prometheus Books, 1996).

Macquarrie, John, _Principles of Christian Theology_ (London, England: SCM Press, 1966).

Main, John, _Silence and Stillness in Every Season: Daily Readings with John Main_, ed. Paul Harris (New York, New York, USA: Continuum, 1997).

Maritain, Jacques, _Education at the Crossroads_ (London, England: Yale University Press, 1943).

Masefield, John, *Spunyarn: Sea Poetry and Prose*, ed. Philip W. Errington (London, England: Penguin Books, 2011).

McBrien, Richard, *Catholicism* (London, England: Geoffrey Chapman, 1994).

Merton, Thomas, *Thoughts in Solitude* (New York, New York, USA: Farrar, Straus and Giroux, 1999).

Mitchell, Stephen, ed., *The Enlightened Heart: An Anthology of Sacred Poetry* (New York, New York, USA: HarperPerennial, 1993).

Moriarty, John, *Nostos: An Autobiography* (Dublin, Ireland, Lilliput Press, 2001).

Morley, Janet, *All Desires Known* (New York, New York, USA: Morehouse Publishing, 1994).

Motion, Andrew, *Selected Poems: 1976–1997* (London, England: Faber & Faber, 2002).

O'Connell, Eugene, *One Clear Call: A Collection of Poetry* (Cork, Ireland: Bradshaw Books, 2003).

O'Driscoll, Dennis, *Stepping Stones: Interviews with Seamus Heaney* (London, England: Faber & Faber, 2008).

Okri, Ben, *Birds of Heaven* (London, England: Weidenfeld & Nicolson, 1995).

Oliver, Mary, *Dream Work* (New York, New York, USA: Atlantic Monthly Press, 1986).

Oliver, Mary, *Swan: Poems and Prose Poems* (Boston, Massachusetts, USA: Beacon Press, 2010).

Oliver, Mary, *Why I Wake Early* (Boston, Massachusetts, USA: Beacon Press, 2004).

O'Murchu, Diarmuid, *In the Beginning was the Spirit: Science, Religion, and Indigenous Spirituality* (Maryknoll, New York, USA: Orbis Books, 2012).

Paul, S.K., *The Complete Poems of Rabindranath Tagore's* Gitanjali: *Texts and Critical Evaluation* (New Delhi, National Capital Territory of Delhi, India: Sarup, 2006).

Rahner, Karl, *The Eternal Year* (London, England: Burns & Oates, 1991).

Rahner, Karl, *Theological Investigations* (New York, New York, USA: Crossroad, 1973).

Raine, Kathleen, *Selected Poems* (Great Barrington, Massachusetts, USA: Lindisfarne Press, 1988).

Roberts, Lynn, *Rosa Mundi* (InVerse, 2011).

Roberts, Michael Symmons, *Corpus* (London, England: Jonathan Cape, 2004).

Rohr, Richard, *The Naked Now: Learning to See as the Mystics See* (New York, New York, USA: Crossroad, 2009).

Rupp, Joyce, *May I Have This Dance?* (Notre Dame, Indiana, USA: Ave Maria Press, 1992).

Sarton, May, *Collected Poems: 1930–1993* (New York, New York, USA: W. W. Norton, 1993).

Schmemann, Alexander, *For the Life of the World* (Crestwood, New York, USA: St Vladimir's Seminary Press, 1973).

Segundo, Juan Luis, *Evolution and Guilt* (Maryknoll, New York, USA: Orbis Books, 1974).

Skelley, Michael, *The Liturgy of the World: Karl Rahner's Theology of Worship* (Collegeville, Minnesota, USA: Liturgical Press, 1991).

Smith, P. R., *Great Moments of Sportsmanship & Extraordinary Sports People* (London, England: P. R. Smith, 2008).

Sölle, Dorothee, *Thinking about God: An Introduction to Theology* (London, England: SCM Press, 1990).

Swimme, Brian, *The Hidden Heart of the Cosmos: Humanity and the New Story* (Maryknoll, New York, USA: Orbis Books, 1996).

Teilhard de Chardin, Pierre, *Hymn of the Universe* (London, England: Collins, 1966).

Teilhard de Chardin, Pierre, *The Divine Milieu*, tr. Siôn Cowell (Brighton, East Sussex, England: Sussex Academic Press, 2004).

Thomas, Dylan, *Selected Poems: 1934–1952* (New York, New York, USA: New Directions, 2003).

Thomas, R. S., *Collected Later Poems 1988–2000* (Tarset, Northumberland, England: Bloodaxe Books, 2004).

Thomas, R. S., *Selected Poems* (London, England: Hachette, 1996).

Thomas, R.S., *The Minister* (Newtown, Powys, Wales: Montgomeryshire Printing Company, 1953).

Whyte, David, *The House of Belonging* (Langley, Washington, USA: Many Rivers Press, 1997).

Whyte, David, *Where Many Rivers Meet* (Langley, Washington, USA: Many Rivers Press, 1990).

Wilder, Thornton, *The Ides of March* (London, England: Penguin Books, 1964).

Williams, H. A., *True Resurrection* (Springfield, Illinois, USA: Templegate, 1983).

Woodruff, Sue, *Meditations with Mechtild of Magdeburg* (Santa Fe, New Mexico, USA: Bear, 1982).